Exploring Mathematics

Activities for
Concept and Skill Development

DISCRETE MATH TEAM
LINCOLN SCHOOL
87 RICHELIEU TER
NEWARK NJ 07106

Exploring Mathematics

Activities for Concept and Skill Development

Grades 4–6

Jean M. Shaw
The University of Mississippi

Scott, Foresman and Company
Glenview, Illinois   London

Good Year Books

are available for preschool through grade 12 and for every basic curriculum subject plus many enrichment areas. For more Good Year Books, contact your local bookseller or educational dealer. For a complete catalog with information about other Good Year Books, please write:

Good Year Books
Department GYB
1900 East Lake Avenue
Glenview, Illinois 60025

7 8 9 10 11 MAL 99 98 97 96 95

ISBN 0-673-18812-4

CONTENTS

From *Exploring Mathematics: Activities for Concept and Skill Development,* Copyright © 1990 Scott, Foresman and Company.

Preface

One of the great needs in U. S. education today is improved instruction in mathematics. Colleges are requiring a greater number and sophistication of math courses for admission, and more and more occupations—as well as life experiences—are demanding math competence.

Effective mathematics education begins in the elementary school, and the intermediate grades (4-6) constitute a crucial time for students to develop math concepts and skills. It is during these years that students must come to understand important mathematical ideas and refine their skills for quick, accurate work in the subject.

Students in the intermediate grades deal with an increasingly wide range of numbers. They explore and learn to handle whole numbers that are larger than they were exposed to in the primary grades. They also begin formal work with rational numbers (fractions and decimals), thereby expanding their number content. Students learn the many similarities and differences between rational numbers and whole numbers.

Complementing their work with numbers, students in the intermediate grades are expected to gain proficiency in computation. They must master basic facts using four operations with whole numbers, and they must extend their skills to working multi-digit problems. It is in the intermediate grades, moreover, that students begin formal work with rational number operations.

Closely related to an expanded facility with numbers and operations is problem solving, which often involves the appropriate application of number skills. Students need work with both routine and nonroutine problems. As they deal with groups of numbers, students need opportunities to organize data. Experiences with simple statistics and graphics can help them make sense of—and interpret—situations that involve numerical data.

Classroom work with calculators complements work in both computation and problem solving. Through carefully planned experiences, students can learn how to use a calculator wisely and recognize that thinking is inseparable from using a calculator correctly.

Finally, students in the intermediate grades need work with measurement and geometry. Some of this work is numerical, but other aspects of it allow students to explore relationships, shapes, and sizes of things in the world around them.

Purpose of This Book

Exploring Mathematics: Activities for Concept and Skill Development, Grades 4-6 presents activities designed to promote students' understanding of important mathematical ideas as well as provide learning experiences intended to let students practice and refine their skills. Concept and skill development are inseparable; they complement each other. Understanding without skill is as incomplete as skill without understanding.

Although this book is intended as a sourcebook for teachers of mathematics in grades four through six, teachers of advanced students in the primary grades will find many of the activities valuable, as will teachers of remedial students in grades seven and eight. Parents may also profit from using the book to provide math enrichment at home, and tutors will likely find many of the book's suggestions useful in their work. Graduate and undergraduate students in elementary education or mathematics education may find much of the book valuable in developing and refining teaching strategies.

Using the Activities

Exploring Mathematics, Grades 4–6 contains many useful materials. Teachers can remove the end-of-the-chapter masters and easily transform these teaching aids into transparencies and worksheets. They can cut out and duplicate the task cards and then distribute these materials to individuals or small groups for independent work. In addition, the book offers suggestions for enhancing math bulletin boards, and it contains patterns for a variety of games to help the busy teacher. In fact, students in the intermediate grades can use the patterns by themselves to prepare some of their own materials.

Each activity in *Exploring Mathematics* is written in an easy-to-use, standardized format. Basic information about each activity alerts the reader to its potential. Objectives tell what the students will do. Instructions for preparing and conducting the activity give the teacher a clear idea of what to do both before and during the exercise. A description of how to evaluate the activity offers ideas on assessing student progress and gathering ideas on student attitudes. This evaluation is intended to help teachers identify students who need extra help on a topic or skill; this help can then be offered through individualized teacher attention, peer tutoring, supplementary textbook or workbook exercises, or other techniques.

Where pertinent, *Exploring Mathematics* provides answers to problems. It even contains answer keys that can be used independently by students. Finally, each activity concludes with extension suggestions—ideas for using the activity in other contexts or using it in a different way to add depth and breadth to children's understanding. These extension suggestions may be used to challenge able students or to provide enrichment and extended work for any interested students.

The activities in *Exploring Mathematics* are suitable for large group work. Often, the instructions suggest breaking the large class into several small groups for parallel work. This technique is very effective for students in the intermediate grades. In the smaller groups, students can help and support each other, and they can share ideas. Mathematics often involves more than one way to solve problems or interpret situations, and small group work allows students to see other points of view. As they work in small groups, students can extend their understandings and skills through working together. Since most of the activities can also be adapted for use by pairs or individuals at their seats or in a learning center, *Exploring Mathematics* allows the teacher to have small groups working on these exercises while the rest of the class does something else.

Development of Concepts, Skills, and Attitudes

Development of positive attitudes toward math—like development of mathematical concepts and skills—will enhance student willingness to work hard, share ideas, and study further. Concepts, skills, and positive attitudes are all best developed through concrete experiences and meaningful materials. Solving practical, real-life problems and working on challenging, unusual problems promote a sense of achievement and positive reinforcement for the effort expended. In addition, successful group experiences help children grow both mentally and socially. *Exploring*

From *Exploring Mathematics: Activities for Concept and Skill Development*, Copyright © 1990 Scott, Foresman and Company.

Mathematics provides varied opportunities for challenging students and encouraging them to develop the necessary concepts, skills, and attitudes for success in mathematics.

A Companion Volume

This book has a companion volume—***Exploring Mathematics: Activities for Concept and Skill Development, Grades K-3.*** Readers who work with fourth graders or remedial students will want to examine that volume as well as this one. The two books share a common organizational format, although the ideas are naturally quite different. Nonetheless, teachers may find the chapters on problem solving and graphing in the primary-level book pertinent to older children. In addition, the chapter in the K-3 book on the wise use of calculators may be appropriate for students in the intermediate grades who have had few (or no) classroom experiences with calculator usage.

Acknowledgments

Many people contributed to the conception and completion of this book. My students and colleagues inspired and challenged me. Charlette Rikard ably typed the manuscript. My children Vicki and Billy encouraged and helped me. I am grateful to all of them for their stimulation and support.

JEAN M. SHAW
OXFORD, MISSISSIPPI

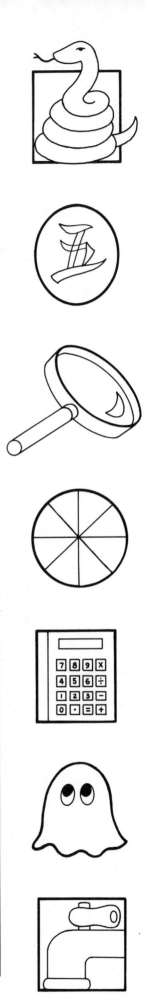

1

Breadth and Depth: Understanding and Using Numbers

In the intermediate grades, children's exposure to numbers expands from dealing with hundreds and thousands to exploring numbers in the millions and beyond. Children examine the place value of large numbers and study large numbers as an extension of the base-ten number system. They not only read, write, and order large numbers, but they also try to understand the meanings of the numbers as well.

To sustain children's attention and interest in the study of numbers, educators must use a variety of activities. In addition to working with large numbers in classroom games and textbook situations, children should also be aware of some uses of large numbers in the world around them. Exploring aspects of the history of numeration systems also contributes to children's knowledge and appreciation of numbers. Effective use of small group work will add to children's motivation to learn about large numbers.

The activities in this chapter offer varied ways to work with numbers and build understanding of their meanings and relative values.

PATTERNS IN CHARTS

Searching for patterns makes use of both mathematics skills and creative thinking. Students use operations and knowledge of numbers as well as generating and testing hypotheses as they discover and verify many kinds of patterns.

Objectives: Students will find and discuss patterns in different kinds of number charts.

Materials: Transparencies to duplicate the charts selected from Teaching Aids 1.1a, b, and c, paper to duplicate charts for students (optional), overhead projector markers.

Preparing for the Activities: Select the charts you want to work with, and make transparencies of the charts. If you wish, you can duplicate copies of the charts for students to discuss as you work.

Conducting the Activities: Project the selected charts on the chalkboard; doing so allows you to circle individual numbers or highlight them as you talk. Lead students in a discussion of the patterns that they see. You might start with a general question like: "What patterns do you see?" Most students will find it easiest to point out the patterns they are discussing if they go up to the chalkboard or projector.

Here are some other questions that are appropriate for most of the charts:

What patterns do you see in the various rows? Columns?

What patterns can you find in the diagonals? (Note that the patterns found in the diagonals that slant from the upper right to the lower left may be different from those that slant from the upper left to the lower right. Note also that each chart has many diagonals parallel to the diagonals from corner to corner.)

What is the sum of the numbers in each row? How do the sums of various row compare? What shortcuts can we find to getting the sums?

Where do odd and even numbers occur in the charts?

Rows of 10 Hundreds Chart (Teaching Aid 1.1a). Locate the odd and even numbers. [They occur in every other column.] Where are the perfect squares? [They're in a diagonal from upper left to lower right.] What patterns do you see in the multiples of 2, 3, 5, 7, and so on? [Patterns will vary; let a student circle each one as other students in the class call them out, and then discuss the patterns.]

Find the prime numbers by working systematically to examine numbers; circle the primes and cross out the composite numbers. Write a star on 1, which is neither prime nor composite. Then let students describe ways to proceed in an efficient manner. (For

From Exploring Mathematics: Activities for Concept and Skill Development, Copyright © 1990 Scott, Foresman and Company.

example, 2 is prime, but all multiples of 2 are composites that can easily be crossed out in columns. Likewise, after 5—which is prime— the remaining multiples of 5 are easy to cross out in columns below 5.) Proceed to cross out multiples of 3 and 7 in a similar way.

This procedure was devised by Erastosthenes, a Greek mathematician. It is called the Sieve of Erastosthenes because the composite numbers, crossed out, "fall through the sieve" while the primes, circled, stay behind. Ask what other patterns the students see in the chart.

Rows of 7 Hundreds Chart (Teaching Aid 1.1b). Compare the patterns that odd and even numbers make in this chart to those found in the rows of 10 chart. Work the Sieve of Erastosthenes procedure and find the patterns of primes in the rows of 7 chart. Have the students compare the rows of 7 chart to a calendar and describe similarities and differences. Compare the first and last number in each row of the rows of 7 chart to the middle number.

Triangular Hundreds Chart (Teaching Aid 1.1c). Have the students find a shortcut for finding the sum of the numbers in each row. [One way is to multiply the middle number by the number of numbers.] Examine the sums by the rows and find a pattern [1, 9, 35, 91, 189, ... One way to interpret this pattern is to note that the sum is the middle number times the odd number—1x1, 3x3, 5x7, 7x13, 9x21, ...]

Evaluating the Activities: Observe each student's interest and ability to find and describe patterns.

Extending the Activities: Invite students to extend any of the charts and see if the patterns they discovered also extend. Encourage interested students to read more about Erastosthenes. Explore patterns found in addition or multiplication tables.

LARGE NUMBER SPINNERS

Versatile number spinners generate large numbers for students to work with.

Objectives: Students will spin large numbers and say, order, round, and compare the numbers.

Materials: Paper to duplicate number spinners and place-value charts from Teaching Aid 1.2a, b, c, posterboard, ruler, scissors, glue, large paper clips, brads.

Preparing for the Activity: Duplicate the number spinner and place-value chart patterns. Mount each pattern on a 20x30cm (8x12-inch) piece of posterboard. Duplicate three or four sets of numeral cards. Use a brad to attach a paper clip into the center of each spinner. Make sure that the paper clip spins freely.

Conducting the Activity: Have the students take turns spinning numbers and completing activities. Here are some activities you can use:

Spin a number. Say it. Compare it to 500 000. Is it larger, smaller, or equal to 500 000?

Spin a large number. Arrange numeral cards for the number on the place-value chart. Choose a classmate to say the number.

Spin two numbers. Compare them. Which is larger, or are they equal? Write a number sentence that compares the two numbers. Say the sentence aloud, pronouncing the number names carefully.

Spin a number. Arrange numeral cards to represent the number. Now rearrange or add cards to make 1000 more than the original number, 10 less than the second number, 100 000 more than the third number, and so on.

Spin a number. Round it to the nearest 100 000. Spin a second number. Round it to the nearest 1000, and so on.

Evaluating the Activity: Observe the students' abilities to read, order, and round the numbers they spin.

Extending the Activity: Spin large numbers to use in computation practice. Extend the spinners and place-value charts to include millions or billions. Use exponential notation on the spinners and place-value charts (10^5 for 100 000, 10^4 for 10 000, and so on.)

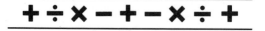

ANCIENT NUMERALS

Exposure to ancient systems of numeration is enriching to students. Work with ancient numerals promotes appreciation of the elegance and simplicity of our modern, base-ten, place-value numeration system.

From *Exploring Mathematics: Activities for Concept and Skill Development*, Copyright © 1990 Scott, Foresman and Company.

Objectives: Students will learn ancient numeral symbols, evaluate numerals expressed in ancient symbols, and express numbers in ancient numerals.

Materials: Paper to reproduce task cards from Teaching Aid 1.3d, transparencies made from Teaching Aid 1.3a, b, and c, overhead projector, scissors.

Preparing for the Activity: Prepare task cards and transparencies.

Conducting the Activity: Show a transparency presenting symbols for one of the ancient numeration systems. Have students take turns using the symbols to express numbers. Let some students write ancient numerals on the chalkboard for their classmates to "decode."

Challenge students to work problems from the task cards. You might present just one system of ancient numerals each day, discussing the advantages and disadvantages of that system before moving on to other systems on subsequent days.

Here are the answers to the problems on Teaching Aid 1.3a, b, c, d.

Transparencies

Egyptian   1. 12 584
          2. ??? ∩∩∩∩∩ //

Chinese   1. 285 , 39
          2. 八 十 五
          3. 二 百 四 十 七

Roman   1. 5392
          2. CXXXIV

Task Cards
1. 𝔁𝔁𝔁𝔁 ???? ∩∩∩∩
       ??? ∩∩∩∩

2. ????? ∩∩∩∩∩ ////
   ????   ///

3. 8500
4. 47
5. 1765

Chinese
1. 刀 百 四 十
2. 八 十 五
3. 734
4. 200
5. 999

Roman I
1. V̄M CDXCVIII
2. X̄ CDXXVI
3. 1234
4. 20 749
5. 515

Roman II
1. CD XXXIX
2. MMM CMXVIII
3. 264
4. 10 895
5. 999

Evaluating the Activity: Check student work, noting whether students were able to draw, express, and decode the ancient numeral symbols correctly. Assess student discussion: Do the students understand the advantages and disadvantages of the various number systems? Determine whether students are eager to work on problems using ancient numerals.

Extending the Activity: Let students create their own task cards for the Chinese, Roman, and Egyptian number systems. Select students to research other ancient or foreign numeration systems and share their findings with classmates. Make a large monthly calendar and let students fill in each day's date with an ancient numeral.

LARGE NUMBER MEANINGS

Students in the intermediate grades deal with large numbers, but many still need work on the meanings of those large numbers. These activities help children develop concrete pictures of such numbers.

Objectives: Students will use paper squares to represent the meanings of large numbers.

Materials: Paper to reproduce counters from Teaching Aid 1.4, scissors, bulletin board backing and letters.

Preparing for the Activities: Duplicate two or three copies of the counters for each student. Prepare a bulletin board space with the caption "See It, Say It."

Conducting the Activities: Have the students examine and discuss the pictures on their sheets, and then have them cut the pieces apart. Ask them how many small squares are in each part. [The smallest square is 1. The other parts show 10, 100, 1000, and 10 000.] Discuss how you might determine how many small squares are in the 1000 and 10 000 pieces without counting. [Students might count the squares in one section and then multiply that number by the number of sections. They might also count the squares in both a row and a column and then find their product.]

From *Exploring Mathematics: Activities for Concept and Skill Development,* Copyright © 1990 Scott, Foresman and Company.

Have the students work in groups of four or five and pool their pieces. Let group members take turns arranging pieces and telling what number is represented. Have the students do some "trading" of pieces as they work. If they arrange twelve 1000 pieces, for example, they can trade ten of the pieces for one 10 000 piece.

After the students are familiar with representing numbers with the pieces, do some other activities such as the following:

Represent two numbers (perhaps using numbers from your textbook), and then write the numerals for the numbers. Read aloud a number sentence about the numbers represented.

Represent three or four numbers and then put them in order from largest to smallest or smallest to largest.

Represent numbers such as 1 less than 10 000, 2000 more than 7256, 10 more than 9990, or 1000 less than 12 750.

Have each group add to a "See It, Say It" bulletin board. Group members should write out the words for a four- or five-digit number and then display the pieces to represent the number below it. Collect the remaining pieces for subsequent group or individual use.

Evaluating the Activities: Circulate among the students and observe them as they work. Notice who understands number relationships and who needs more help with concrete aids. Also note who assumes a leadership role in discussions and manipulation of pieces.

Extending the Activities: Use the pieces to represent numbers generated with number cubes (Teaching Aid 2.1a) and number spinners. Lead students to decide how many 10 000 pieces they would need to represent numbers such as one million, two billion, or three trillion.

WRITE, ORDER, WORK

Objectives: Students write numbers that are presented orally, put the numbers in order, and perform computations with the numbers.

Materials: Chalkboard and chalk.

Conducting the Activity: Organize students into five or six teams of approximately equal ability. If students sit in rows, consider making each row a team. Start by having one member from each team go to the chalkboard. Then different team members go up in turns, working through the following steps:

Write the numeral that the teacher calls out (e.g., "three thousand eighty").

Write the second numeral that the teacher calls out.

Write the third numeral that the teacher calls out.

Write the fourth numeral that the teacher calls out.

Read a numeral or two.

Recopy the numerals in order.

Perform a computation on the numerals. (Add them, subtract the smallest from the largest, add only the odd numbers, multiply the smallest by 1000, etc.)

You might award points for each step. One scoring method is to give two points to the first student who finishes correctly (the student could turn around to indicate when he or she is through). Give one point to every other student who gets the correct answer. For the computation step, you might also ask all students (including the seated ones) to perform the computations, and then award a point for *each* correct answer. Keep the game moving quickly.

Evaluating the Activity: Notice whether students work quietly and cooperatively. Also note each student's ability to write and read numerals. Determine which students can order numerals and perform computations accurately.

Extending the Activity: Encourage students to suggest other activities they might do with numbers you call out. Let students take turns dictating numbers for others to write and order.

From *Exploring Mathematics: Activities for Concept and Skill Development,* Copyright © 1990 Scott, Foresman and Company.

÷ ✕ − ✛ − ✕ ÷

CHAPTER

1

TEACHING

AIDS

÷ ✕ − ✛ − ✕ ÷

1	2	3	4	5	6	7	8	9	10
11	12	13	14	15	16	17	18	19	20
21	22	23	24	25	26	27	28	29	30
31	32	33	34	35	36	37	38	39	40
41	42	43	44	45	46	47	48	49	50
51	52	53	54	55	56	57	58	59	60
61	62	63	64	65	66	67	68	69	70
71	72	73	74	75	76	77	78	79	80
81	82	83	84	85	86	87	88	89	90
91	92	93	94	95	96	97	98	99	100

TEN BY TEN HUNDREDS CHART

From Exploring Mathematics: Activities for Concept and Skill Development, Copyright © 1990 Scott, Foresman and Company.

Teaching Aid 1.1a

7 COLUMN HUNDREDS CHART

1	2	3	4	5	6	7
8	9	10	11	12	13	14
15	16	17	18	19	20	21
22	23	24	25	26	27	28
29	30	31	32	33	34	35
36	37	38	39	40	41	42
43	44	45	46	47	48	49
50	51	52	53	54	55	56
57	58	59	60	61	62	63
64	65	66	67	68	69	70
71	72	73	74	75	76	77
78	79	80	81	82	83	84
85	86	87	88	89	90	91
92	93	94	95	96	97	98
99	100	101	102	103	104	105

Teaching Aid 1.1b

TRIANGULAR HUNDREDS CHART

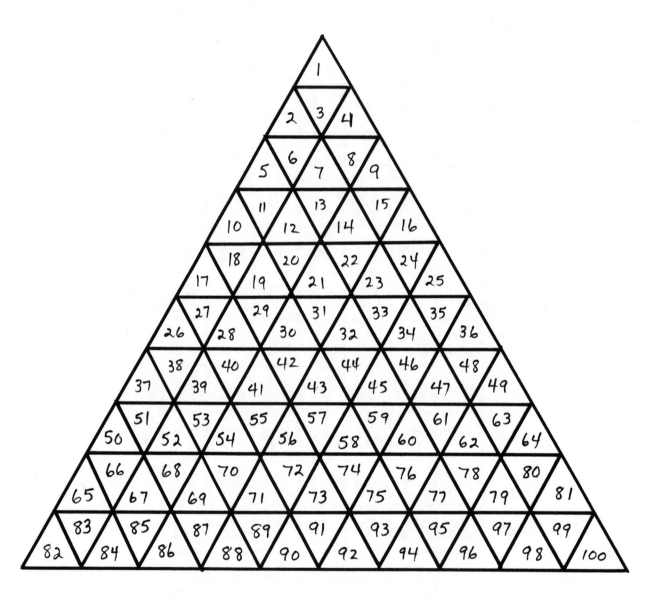

Teaching Aid 1.1c

SPIN A NUMBER

Large Number
Spinner Pattern

Use a brad to attach a
small paper clip to the
center of each section.

thousands
1 000's

ten thousands
10 000's

hundred thousands
100 000's

ones
1's

tens
10's

hundreds
100's

Teaching Aid 1.2a

LARGE NUMBER SPINNER

ONE3

hundreds
100's

tens
10's

ones
1's

7 8 9 0

Children spin a number, then arrange the appropriate number cards in the place value chart.

THOUSANDS			ONES	
8	6	2	5	0

8 6 2 5 0 1

LARGE NUMBER SPINNER.

Place Value Chart
Teaching Aid 1.2c

THOUSANDS

hundred thousands
100 000's

ten thousands
10 000's

one thousand
1 000's

6

5

4

3

2

1

From *Exploring Mathematics: Activities for Concept and Skill Development*, Copyright © 1990 Scott, Foresman and Company.

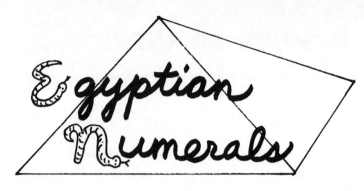

Egyptian Numerals

Symbol	Value	Name
/	1	stroke
∩	10	arch
ℓ	100	coiled rope
↑	1000	lotus flower
↗	10 000	finger
↗	100 000	tadpole

Features
- Based on tens
- No zero symbol
- Put larger valued symbols at the left

$$↑ ℓℓℓℓ ∩∩ //// = 1428$$

Problems
Evaluate

$$⌐ ↑↑ ℓℓℓℓℓ ∩∩∩∩∩∩∩∩ ////$$

Write in Egyptian -- 352

From *Exploring Mathematics: Activities for Concept and Skill Development*, Copyright © 1990 Scott, Foresman and Company.

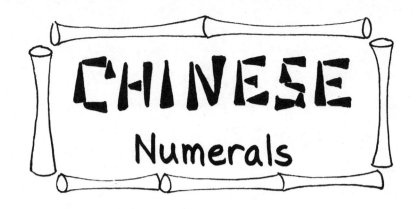

Chinese Numerals

Ciphered Chinese Symbols

一	1	六	6	二十	20
二	2	七	7	三十	30
三	3	八	8	四十	40
四	4	九	9	百	100
五	5	十	10	二百	200

Features

- Symbols for 1-9 and powers of 10.
- Uses adding and multiplying to get values.

四百 = 400

(4 x 100)

五百九十六 = 596

$(5 \times 100) + (9 \times 10) + 6$

Problems

Evaluate:

二百八十五

三十九

Write in Chinese:

85

247

ROMAN NUMERALS

Symbol	Value
I	1
V	5
X	10
L	50
C	100
D	500
M	1000

Features

- Usually larger values are written first.
- A smaller symbol placed before a larger one means subtract smaller from larger
  $$IV = 5 - 1 = 4 \qquad IX = 10 - 9 = 1$$
- A bar over a symbol multiplies its value by 1000
  $$\overline{V} = 5000 \qquad \overline{M} = 1\,000\,000$$
- System based on fives and tens

Problems:

Evaluate $\overline{V}CCCXCII$

Write 134 in Roman numerals

From Exploring Mathematics: Activities for Concept and Skill Development, Copyright © 1990 Scott, Foresman and Company.

CHINESE Numerals

Use your own paper.
Write each in ciphered Chinese

1. 840   2. 65

Decipher these Chinese numerals:

3. 七百三十四
4. 一百
5. 九百九十九

ROMAN Numerals II

Use your own paper.
Write each as a Roman numeral.

1. 439
2. 3918

Express these in modern form:

3. CCLXIV
4. X̄DCCCXCV
5. IM

Egyptian Numerals

Use your own paper.
Write these in Egyptian numerals:

1. 4780   2. 957

What do these mean? Decode them.

3. 𓎃𓎃𓎃 𓏺𓏺𓏺𓏺𓏺
4. ∩∩∩∩ ''''   '''
5. 𓎆 𓏺𓏺𓏺 ∩∩∩ ''''
   ∩∩∩

ROMAN Numerals I

Use your own paper.
Convert these to Roman numerals.

1. 6498
2. 10 426

What do these mean? Write their values:

3. MCCXXXIV
4. XXDCCXLIX
5. DXCV

Task Cards for Ancient Numerals   Teaching Aid 1.3d

LARGE NUMBER PIECES

Cut the 1, 10, and
100 pieces on the
dotted lines so they
will not be lost.

1 ▫

10 ▭

100

1000

10 000

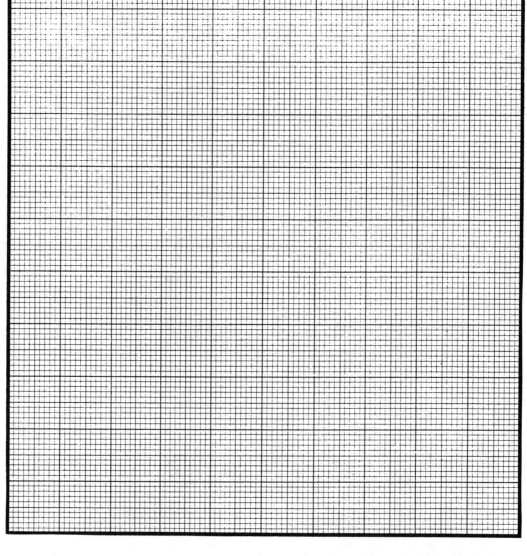

Teaching Aid 1.4

From *Exploring Mathematics: Activities for Concept and Skill Development*, Copyright © 1990 Scott, Foresman and Company.

2
Basic Facts and Operations With Whole Numbers: Computation

The computational needs of students in the fourth through sixth grades vary greatly. Some students still need help mastering basic facts while others need varied opportunities to work with multi-digit computation problems. Students also need situations in which they can work alone, in pairs or small groups, and in large groups.

The activities in this chapter provide several different ways for students to practice basic facts and operations with whole numbers. The activities also relate to materials found in chapters 3, 4, and 6. In Chapter 3, students frequently use computations as they solve problems. The calculator problems in Chapter 4 encourage students to use their minds as well as their calculators to perform computations. In the Chapter 6 activities, students use both number sense and computational abilities as they work with statistics and graphing.

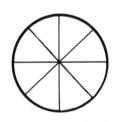

Computations also are important in working with fractions and decimals, area and perimeter, and measurements. Since work with computations extends to virtually every area of mathematics, success in such work is crucial. Use the activities in this chapter to build skills and to motivate students.

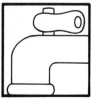

NUMBER CUBES

Roll out the number cubes for variety, suspense, and interest in computation practice!

Objectives: Students will construct number cubes and use the cubes in a variety of computation problems.

Materials: Paper to duplicate number and message cubes (Teaching Aids 2.1a and b), scissors, glue.

Preparing for the Activity: Duplicate one or two number cube patterns (Teaching Aid 2.1a) for each student. Duplicate one "Roll a Message" cube pattern (Teaching Aid 2.1b) for each group of four or five students.

Conducting the Activity: Instruct students to write six numbers from 0 to 9 at random on the faces of the blank cube patterns. Students who need more practice with "harder" facts may write the numbers from 5 to 9 and 0 on their cubes.

   Then have the students cut out the cubes and neatly glue them together. Divide the class into small groups and have the children use their cubes for computation practice according to the following formats:

   Roll two cubes and find the sum or product of the numbers that come up on top.

   Roll two cubes and write down the numbers that come up on top as a two-digit number. Then reverse the digits to make another two-digit number. Subtract the smaller from the larger number.

   Roll three cubes. Use the three digits that come up on top to make all possible three-digit numbers. For example, if a 2, 5, and 9 come up, the six three-digit numbers that can be made are 259, 295, 529, 592, 925, and 952. Place the numbers in order from smallest to largest. Find their average.

   Using three cubes, roll a three-digit number and see if it is divisible by 2, 3, 5, and/or 10.

   Using the message cube and two number cubes, throw the number cubes to determine a two-digit number, and then complete the problem from the message cube.

   Use the message cube with three or four number cubes to create and then solve computational problems.

Evaluating the Activity: Have the students check each other by hand or with the help of a calculator. Spot-check each child's work and determine who works with ease and who needs some individual help.

Extending the Activity: Have the students create number games using the cubes.

From *Exploring Mathematics: Activities for Concept and Skill Development*, Copyright © 1990 Scott, Foresman and Company.

VIEW A FACT

These handy viewers are easy to make and can be personalized to fit each child's needs. As the children use the viewers, they receive immediate feedback on the accuracy of their answers.

Objectives: Students will practice basic facts and check their own answers.

Materials: Paper to reproduce viewers from Teaching Aid 2.2, stapler and staples, scissors.

Preparing for the Activity: Prepare the viewers yourself or have the students do it. Prepare problem-answer strips (each student can tell you in advance what facts he or she needs to practice). The easiest way to prepare the strips is to write a problem, turn the strip over, and immediately write the answer; then write the next problem and answer.

Conducting the Activity: Have the students work in pairs, one reading and answering the problems as quickly as possible while the other checks the answers. Then have them reverse roles. If you want, you can have the children keep track of the proportion of correct answers.

Evaluating the Activity: Observe to see whether the children work cooperatively and stay on task. What proportion of correct answers did each student achieve? Are students making progress?

Extending the Activity: Use geometric shapes, time clocks, coins and values, and equivalent fractions in the question-answer strips. Encourage children to use their viewers in their spare time or at home. Have the children use one of the forms in Teaching Aid 2.3a or b to keep track of their results when using the fact viewers.

FACT SEARCHES

Like word searches, fact searches intrigue youngsters and motivate them to look carefully for basic facts hidden in a grid.

Objective: Students will circle basic facts found in a fact search grid.

Materials: Paper to duplicate the fact search worksheets (Teaching Aid 2.4a and b).

Preparing for the Activity: Duplicate copies of the fact searches.

Conducting the Activity: Show the students how to locate basic facts in the grid. They should circle the facts they find and write in the correct operation signs and equals signs. Have the students check each other's work and help classmates locate unmarked facts.
    Here are the answers to Teaching Aid 2.4a and b.

2.4a   2.4b

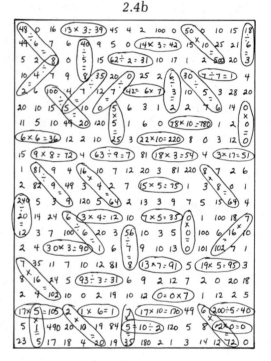

Evaluating the Activity: Spot-check students' work, noting who locates basic facts quickly and who needs more work in recognizing facts.

Extending the Activity: Encourage interested students to make their own fact searches for their classmates or for younger children. Present the "Calculating Crostics" activity from Chapter 4.

WORK, LIFT, AND CHECK

These easily made devices permit quick practice of basic facts and mental arithmetic problems. Because they let students check their work almost instantly, the devices provide immediate feedback.

Objectives: Students will practice basic facts and mental arithmetic problems using work, lift, and check devices.

Materials: Paper to duplicate the work, lift, and check devices from Teaching Aids 2.5a, b, c, and d, scissors, glue.

Preparing for the Activity: Choose the work, lift, and check format you would like to use. Duplicate a copy for each child.

Conducting the Activity: Help students cut out and construct the work, lift, and check devices. Have them either work with their own devices or exchange devices with classmates. Then set aside several minutes each day to work on basic facts, using the work, lift, and check devices for at least a portion of this practice period.

Evaluating the Activity: Observe the children as they work, noting the neatness of their work as well as their success in using the fact practice devices.

Extending the Activity: Have interested students design different types of work, lift, and check devices. Arrange for interested students to make devices with simple problems and use the devices with younger children in tutoring sessions.

OVERHEAD FACT PRACTICE

Use the overhead projector to show many facts in a hurry and with little effort. This activity demands students' attention and on-task behavior.

Objectives: Students will say or write answers to basic facts shown on the overhead projector.

Materials: Transparencies, paper to make masking sheets, overhead projector.

Preparing for the Activity: Make a transparency from Teaching Aid 2.6. Prepare "masking sheets" as described and shown below. These masking sheets will let you reveal just the right number of digits for problems.

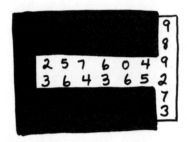

To show 2 addends or factors, cut a 4 cm section from a masking sheet. Move the sheet along to reveal problems.

Conducting the Activity: Arrange the masking sheet over the random number transparency so that the numbers show. State the operation that the students will be practicing. Have the students either say the answers in unison or write five to ten answers on scratch paper and then quickly check their answers before practicing more facts. Keep these sessions of overhead fact practice short and active.

Evaluating the Activity: Observe the students and determine who seems able to follow along and who needs more practice.

Extending the Activity: Let small groups of students do this activity independently. As they work, group members should make note of facts that cause them problems so that they can practice these facts some more later. Make a masking sheet to show four- or five-digit numbers. Have the students pronounce or round off when you reveal the numbers.

From *Exploring Mathematics: Activities for Concept and Skill Development,* Copyright © 1990 Scott, Foresman and Company.

÷ ✕ — + — ✕ ÷

CHAPTER

2

TEACHING

AIDS

÷ ✕ — + — ✕ ÷

NUMBER CUBE PATTERN

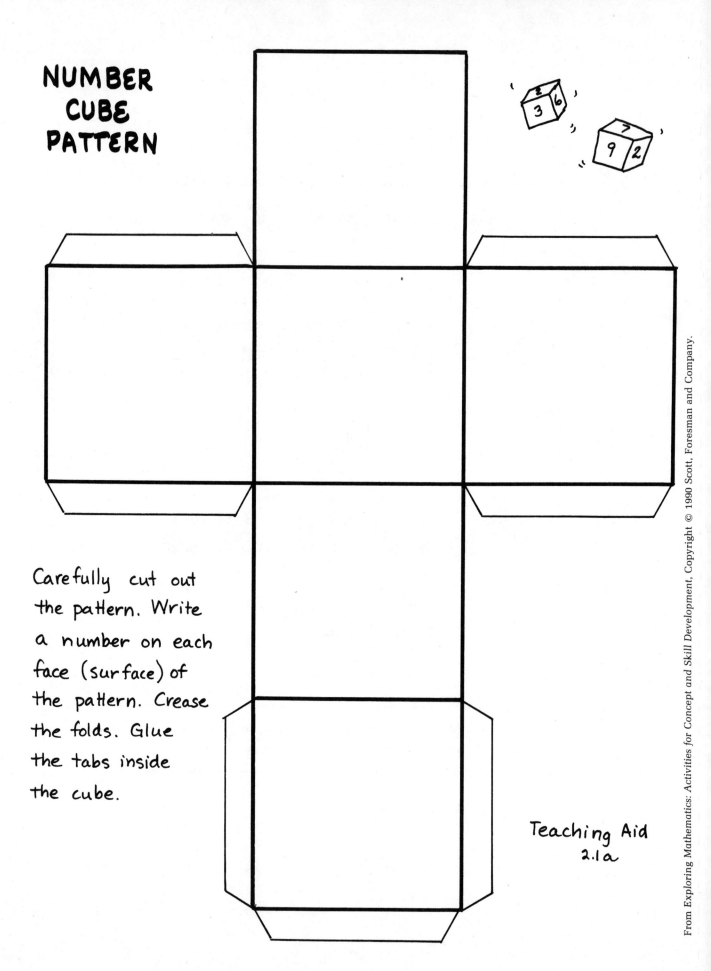

Carefully cut out the pattern. Write a number on each face (surface) of the pattern. Crease the folds. Glue the tabs inside the cube.

Teaching Aid
2.1a

From Exploring Mathematics: Activities for Concept and Skill Development, Copyright © 1990 Scott, Foresman and Company.

MESSAGE CUBE PATTERN

Roll four numbers. Find their average.

Roll a number. Subtract it from 10000.

Roll two numbers. Double the smaller number. Multiply the result by the larger number.

Roll a number. Multiply it by itself.

Roll two numbers. Multiply each number by 10.

Carefully cut out the pattern. Crease each fold. Glue the tabs inside the cube.

Double the number shown.

Teaching Aid 2.1b

VIEW A FACT
pattern

Problems

Answers

← staple here →

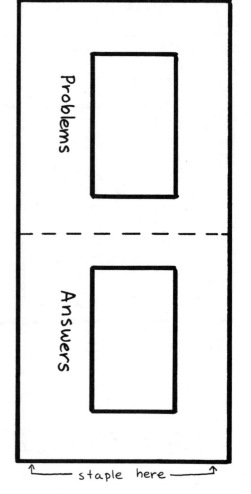

Cut out and fold
the viewer.
Staple it along
the edge.
Decorate the
opening if you like.
Write problems
on the lines. Write
answers on the
back. Insert the
problem strip.
Pull it through the viewer to see
each problem and answer.

front	back
8×4	32
7×6	42
7×8	56
9×6	54
8×8	64
9×9	81
7×9	63
8×6	48
9×6	54
7×7	49

Teaching Aid 2.2

Record Form -- Fact Practice

MAKE YOUR THERMOMETER HIT THE TOP!

PERFECT!

GOOD WORK!

OK WORK

NOT SO GOOD-- KEEP WORKING!

10
9
8
Number 7
of
Correct 6
Answers
Per 5
Each 10
Problems 4
Tried
3
2
1
0

Dates _ _ _ _

Recording Form for FACT PRACTICE

name _____

Date	Number of Facts Tried	Number of Facts Answered Right	Fraction of Facts Answered Right	Progress Code *

* Improved over last day's work   Same as last day's work 😦 Score down from last day's work

Teaching Aid 2.3b

From *Exploring Mathematics: Activities for Concept and Skill Development*, Copyright © 1990 Scott, Foresman and Company.

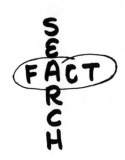

At least 40 addition and subtraction facts are hidden below. They may be displayed across, up and down, or diagonally. Ring each fact. Write in a + or − sign and = sign. An example is done for you.

25	7	5	8	10	2	20	30	11	0	11	11	6	47	0	17
0	12	8	5	13	0	19	4	⟨15 = 8 + 7⟩		12	8	5	8	14
7	10	13	9	4	9	9	8	4	12	39	10	14	9	12	6
1	7	6	1	9	3	10	3	30	0	5	10	5	17	22	1
13	4	9	6	9	30	21	31	12	6	9	17	10	28	5	15
2	8	41	0	18	3	40	9	42	9	16	6	30	38	13	8
4	27	8	9	5	2	23	10	13	8	8	0	4	11	13	9
6	13	2	9	29	0	41	7	5	0	8	7	37	8	19	17
3	14	7	10	2	12	7	4	20	14	12	50	3	19	3	6
40	19	21	5	10	22	18	16	12	7	8	30	44	14	13	1
1	8	5	15	3	12	0	15	8	13	10	20	7	19	5	18
9	5	42	0	6	0	22	7	15	7	3	8	1	10	2	8
4	7	2	32	4	14	36	2	6	45	8	9	43	11	5	17
2	12	7	12	16	1	23	10	46	9	2	6	12	0	1	13
16	5	33	1	35	36	50	8	5	14	6	8	17	0	8	25
2	6	11	4	1	0	5	2	42	5	4	10	12	1	7	3
5	1	22	0	34	15	11	9	13	0	48	20	28	5	1	32
3	9	11	49	14	6	8	1	9	11	3	30	12	18	2	7
9	0	14	2	24	9	3	5	9	2	2	33	6	26	11	14
11	1	3	15	18	4	10	3	10	0	7	19	0	16	15	1
13	12	9	19	45	13	5	8	12	4	8	5	3	29	1	10

Teaching Aid 2.4a

FACT SEARCH

At least 50 facts are hidden in the numbers below. The multiplication and division facts may be hidden across, up and down, or diagonally. Draw around each fact and write in ×, ÷, and = signs. One example is done for you.

48	0	16	13	3	39	45	4	2	100	0	50	0	10	15	18
49	6	7	6	40	9	5	0	14	3	42	15	10	25	21	6
5	2	8	0	5	15	62	2	31	10	17	1	2	500	20	3
10	4	7	9	8	35	20	0	25	2	6	30	7	7	1	4
2	6	100	4	7	12	7	42	6	7	3	10	5	3	28	20
20	10	15	5	10	0	5	6	3	1	2	2	7	6	14	0
11	5	10	49	20	120	5	1	6	0	78	10	780	1	2	0
6	6	36	12	2	10	25	3	22	10	220	8	0	3	12	0
15	9	8	72	4	63	9	7	81	18	3	54	4	3	17	51
1	81	9	4	16	10	7	12	20	3	81	220	8	7	2	6
2	82	9	49	3	4	2	7	15	5	75	1	3	8	0	1
240	5	3	9	120	5	64	2	13	3	9	7	5	15	64	4
20	14	24	6	3	4	12	10	7	5	35	0	1	100	18	7
12	3	7	100	6	20	3	56	10	3	5	0	100	6	16	10
2	4	30	3	90	1	6	7	9	10	13	0	101	102	7	1
7	35	11	7	10	12	81	8	13	7	91	5	19	5	95	3
8	16	24	5	93	3	31	6	9	2	12	7	2	0	20	18
2	4	102	10	0	2	19	10	12	0	0	7	1	12	2	5
17	5	105	2	1	6	1	7	17	10	170	49	6	200	5	40
5	1	490	20	10	19	84	5	10	2	120	5	8	12	0	0
23	5	17	18	4	20	19	35	180	2	1	3	14	12	72	0

The circled example reads: 50 × 10 = 500

Teaching Aid 2.4b

Work, Lift, Check

Teaching Aid 2.5a

Cut the patterns on the heavy lines.
Crease them on the dotted lines. Glue
the bottom sections with the answers underneath.

WORK, LIFT, CHECK

Work each problem mentally.
Lift the flap and check your answer.

| 8 | 25 | 40 | 2)30 | 17 | 40 | 51 | 3)81 |
| +15 | −12 | ×2 | | +23 | −17 | ×3 | |

WORK, LIFT, CHECK

Multiply each number by 6.
Lift the flap to check your answer.

| 8 | 11 | 3 | 9 | 12 | 7 | 20 | 6 |

Make your own Work, Lift, Check. Cut the patterns along the heavy lines. Crease the problem section on the dotted lines. Glue the answer section underneath. Write problems on the flaps. Write in answers on the answer section. Try to say the answers, then lift the flaps to check yourself.

WORK, LIFT, CHECK

Problems

Answers

Write answers to your problems in the blanks.

Teaching Aid 2.5b

From Exploring Mathematics: Activities for Concept and Skill Development, Copyright © 1990 Scott, Foresman and Company.

WORK, LIFT, AND CHECK
Problem Pattern

Cut out the form on the heavy lines.
Crease it on the dotted lines. Cut out the
answer section. Glue the top to the
bottom answer section by gluing the center
only. Write problems on the top. Write
answers on the bottom. Exchange
problems with classmates
and let them work
your problems.

Teaching Aid 2.5c

WORK, LIFT, AND CHECK
Answer Pattern

this is the answer section for your Work, Lift, and Check problems. Cut it out along the heavy lines. Put glue on the center. Glue the answer section under the problem section. Write answers after you write the problems.

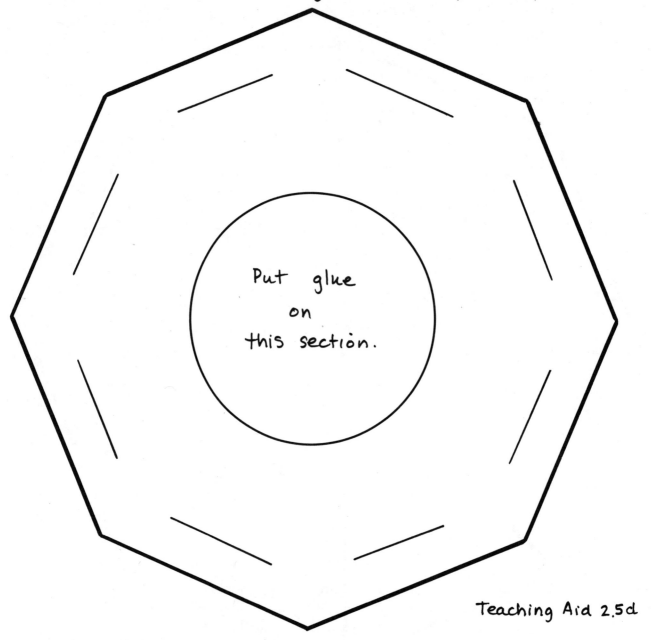

Put glue
on
this section.

Teaching Aid 2.5d

From Exploring Mathematics: Activities for Concept and Skill Development, Copyright © 1990 Scott, Foresman and Company.

5	1	7	7	2	7	4	6	4
0	4	2	3	3	1	2	9	0
4	4	4	6	6	2	1	6	2
8	9	8	9	3	5	8	2	0
4	1	8	6	1	9	6	4	0
8	7	0	5	6	2	4	0	3
3	2	3	4	9	1	8	3	5
8	7	0	6	5	6	8	2	1
9	6	0	4	5	9	3	9	6
0	1	7	3	9	5	8	6	3

Teaching Aid 2.6   Random Number Chart

3

Understand, Solve, and Check: Problem Solving

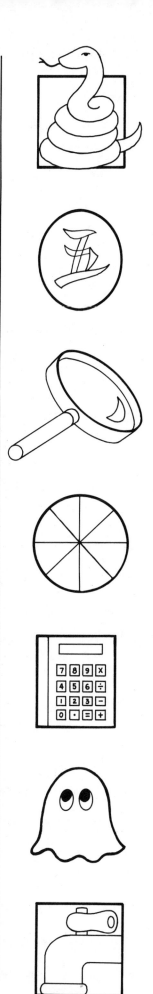

Problem solving—or the application of knowledge in new situations—is important for students in the intermediate grades. As they work with problem solving, students must gain insight into problems: What is given? What is being asked? They must then plan and carry out solutions to problems.

Sometimes students find that a trial-and-error strategy is appropriate, trying a method and then checking themselves. At other times, they may find it valuable to examine a problem for patterns or to look carefully at pictures, charts, or graphs. One procedure, however, is constant: The final step in problem solving is checking. Does the answer make sense? Does it address the question that was asked? Is it approximately or exactly correct?

Besides encountering the word problems in their textbooks, students need exposure to nonroutine problems or ones that require thought and selection of an appropriate strategy to solve them. Students also need to work with real-world problems, the kind that lets them see the value of problem solving in their lives. In some cases, students should work by themselves to solve problems, but they also need to spend some time working in groups. Adults often solve problems in committees and other groups, recognizing that many heads can be better than one in finding solutions to complicated problems.

The problems in this chapter are varied. Many use numbers, but some are built around spatial relationships. Students can tackle these problems alone or in groups, and they can work the problems in several different ways. Discussion of ways to think about the problems and ways to find the answers will be productive. Whether used as a regular assignment or offered as an enrichment, the following activities will challenge and intrigue students in the intermediate grades.

PUZZLE CORNER

Challenge your students with all kinds of problems and puzzles by establishing a regular display in a designated area of your room.

Objectives: Students will try to solve problems involving numbers, relationships, geometric shapes, and logical reasoning.

Materials: Paper to duplicate problems (Teaching Aid 3.1a, b, c, d, e, f, g) and answers (Teaching Aid 3.2), materials to construct a puzzle corner area.

Preparing for the Activity: Decorate a small area of the classroom for a puzzle corner. You might use a section of a bulletin board, a carrel, or part of a table top. Duplicate selected puzzles and display them a few at a time in the puzzle corner.

Conducting the Activity: Show students the puzzle corner and invite them to work on the problems you have posted there. Emphasize that solving the problems will involve creative work and that they should check their answers before considering their problem-solving practice complete. Set up a procedure for verifying answers. Students might check answers with you, use an answer key posted in the puzzle corner, or check answers with a student you have designated as "helper of the week."

   Encourage students to try new problems even though they may not have succeeded with previous ones. Vary the types of problems you present, thereby tapping different problem-solving abilities and strategies. From time to time, discuss the various strategies that students use to solve problems. In addition, periodically ask students to contribute problems to the puzzle corner.

   To recognize students who successfully solve problems, you might award stickers or stars. Among other means of recognition you could use is creation of an "I Solved It!" list to which you allow students to add their names.

Evaluating the Activity: Observe the students' work. Note who regularly completes problems, who works persistently, and who expresses good ideas regarding problem-solving strategies.

Extending the Activity: Organize a problem-solving contest, perhaps pitting teams in your classroom against teams from other classrooms. Try to involve all your students as contestants, judges, timers, and problem contributors. Add to your problem collection from time to time, and invite students to contribute as well.

2, 3, 4, 5 PROBLEMS

What can you do with four little numbers and all the operation signs you wish? Lots! In this activity, students discover how many other numbers they can express using only a 2, 3, 4, and 5.

Objectives: Students will manipulate numbers and operations to express other numbers. They will use parentheses and exponents in mathematical expressions.

Materials: Paper to duplicate student worksheets (Teaching Aid 3.3).

Preparing for the Activity: Duplicate copies of the worksheet.

Conducting the Activity: Present or review how to use parentheses in mathematical expressions. Emphasize that operations "inside" parentheses are done first.
Try problems like these:

$18 - (5 \times 2)$	[Answer: 8]
$(4 \times 7) - (6 \div 2)$	[Answer: 25]
$(19 + 4) \times 5$	[Answer: 115]
$9 + (4 \times 5)$	[Answer: 29]

If the children are not familiar with exponents, introduce the concept with examples such as $2^2 = 2 \times 2 = 4$ and $8^2 = 8 \times 8 = 64$ and $3^4 = 3 \times 3 \times 3 \times 3 = 81$. Work a few problems with exponents.

Now present the idea that students will use only the numbers 2, 3, 4, and 5 along with any operations and signs they wish to express other numbers. Tell the students that they may use each number only once in an expression. For example, they can use $2 + 3 + 4 + 5 = 14$ and $(5 \times 4) - (2 + 3) = 15$. Let the students present some other expressions and find their values. Some students may find it easier to start on the "free choice" section at problem 26, and some may wish to work in pairs.

Most students will not finish the worksheet in one class period, and you might want to assign it for completion in a week. Do not grade the worksheets; instead, allow the students to compare and discuss their answers.

Here are some possible worksheet answers. Have the students check one another's suggestions, but make clear that answers other than those shown below may be correct.

$$1 = (2 + 5) \div (3 + 4)$$
$$2 = (5 + 3) - (2 + 4)$$
$$3 = (5 + 4) - (2 \times 3)$$
$$4 = (5 + 4) - (2 + 3)$$
$$5 = (3 \times 4) - (2 + 5)$$
$$6 = (5 + 4 + 3) \div 2$$
$$7 = (5 \times 3) - (4 \times 2)$$

$$8 = (5 + 4) - (3 - 2)$$
$$9 = (5 \times 3) - (4 + 2)$$
$$10 = 5 \times (4 + 2) \div 3$$
$$11 = (5 \times 2) + (4 - 3)$$
$$12 = [4 + (5 - 3)] \times 2$$
$$13 = (5 \times 3) - (4 \div 2)$$
$$15 = (5 \times 4) - (2 + 3)$$
$$16 = (4 \times 2) + (5 + 3)$$
$$17 = (5 \times 3) + (4 \div 2)$$
$$18 = 3^2 + (4 + 5)$$
$$19 = (4 \times 3) + (5 + 2)$$
$$20 = [2 \times (5 + 3)] + 4$$
$$21 = (4 \times 5) + (3 - 2)$$
$$22 = (5 \times 2) + (4 \times 3)$$
$$23 = (5 \times 3) + (4 \times 2)$$
$$24 = 5^2 + 3 - 4$$
$$25 = (5 \times 4) + (3 + 2)$$

26. Have students check each other.

Evaluating the Activity: Note student interest and persistence in working the problems. Pay attention to who works cooperatively with others, and see who correctly uses parentheses and exponents as well as accurately executes computations.

Extending the Activity: Encourage students to use other series of numbers for similar activities. Have students use 2, 3, 4, and 5 to express numbers other than those on the worksheet. Let them try to find the highest number that can be made using 2, 3, 4, and 5.

CALENDAR FUN

Put old calendars to good use on these unique problems! This activity is especially fun to do at the start of a new year when outdated calendars are being discarded.

Objectives: Students will follow directions and solve problems based on calendar numbers.

From *Exploring Mathematics: Activities for Concept and Skill Development,* Copyright © 1990 Scott, Foresman and Company.

Materials: Paper to duplicate copies of the task cards from Teaching Aid 3.4a and b for each group of two or three students, old calendar pages.

Preparing for the Activity: Gather old calendar pages or have students bring them in. It makes no difference if the pages are all the same month or different months. Duplicate copies of the task cards.

Conducting the Activity: Organize groups of two or three students. Distribute the task cards among the groups, and have the students work with the cards in whatever order they choose. Let students check their own work as much as possible. Discuss some "calendar magic" results as a large group.

The "Calendar Cutup" answers will vary. Here are the answers to "Calendar Magic":

Block O' Nine. The sum is always three times as great as the center number.

Lightning Addition. The sum always equals seven times the value of the first day plus 21. The second computation always results in the sum of the numbers in a "two-week block."

Sums All Around. Each of the four sums equals three times the center number. The right plus the left column equals six times the middle number. The top row plus the bottom row equals six times the center number!

More Calendar Sums. The sums are the same.

Evaluating the Activity: Circulate around the classroom, spot-checking the students as they work. See who performs computations accurately and who follows directions ably. Determine who takes a leadership role in the problem-solving process.

Extending the Activity: Encourage groups of students to work with calendar pages and try to find other patterns. Invite students to take the calendar magic task cards home with them to share the math tricks with their families. Let interested students research the history of calendars and other time-keeping devices.

NUMBER CLUES

I'm odd, prime, and less than 20. The sum of my digits is 8. What number am I? Students enjoy using number clues to solve mysteries like this and the ones below.

Objectives: Students will work with number clues that include such words as odd, even, prime, multiple, divisible, and perfect squares. They will use the clues and operations to figure out what numbers are being described.

Materials: Paper to duplicate worksheet from Teaching Aid 3.5.

Preparing for the Activity: Duplicate the number clue worksheet.

Conducting the Activity: Present an example or two of number clue problems. You might use these:

1. I am less than 90.
   I'm a multiple of 5.
   The sum of my digits is 9.
   Who am I? [Answer: 45]

2. I'm a multiple of 6.
   I'm less than 100.
   The sum of my digits is 15.
   Each of my digits is divisible by 3.
   Who am I? [Answer: 96]

3. I'm an even number.
   I'm less than 1000 but more than 100.
   Each of my digits is a different number.
   The sum of my digits is 12.
   My hundreds digit is four less than my ones digit.
   My tens digit is two times my hundreds digit.
   Who am I? [Answer: 246]

Let the students work independently for a few minutes. Then conduct a discussion about the problems. Help the students see how each successive clue gives more information and narrows the possible numbers that could be the answer. Encourage students to discuss their various strategies for getting started on and completing the problems.

Following this discussion, have the students work on the worksheet independently or in pairs. Here are the worksheet answers:

1. 45
2. 64
3. 311
4. 84
5. 79
6. 120
7. 625

From *Exploring Mathematics: Activities for Concept and Skill Development*, Copyright © 1990 Scott, Foresman and Company.

Evaluating the Activity: Have the students check their own work and discuss some of the clues they used to solve the problems. See who has correct answers and who makes insightful comments.

Extending the Activity: Allow interested students to create similar problems for the class. Invent number clue problems for fractions, decimals, and geometric shapes.

LABEL LINGO

Food package labels contain much valuable information that students—and adults—need to know about. Reading and interpreting labels is a skill that everyone should possess.

Objectives: Students will read and analyze labels that present several problems to solve.

Materials: Paper to reproduce worksheets from Teaching Aid 3.6a and b, scissors, glue, bulletin board backing and signs (suggested on Teaching Aid 3.6c), labels from food products, transparencies.

Preparing for the Activity: Reproduce the worksheets and gather several labels from cans and boxes (students could bring these). Prepare the bulletin board (except for the arrows) and the transparencies.

Conducting the Activity: Before showing the labels to the class, ask students what information the labels might contain. Verify student responses by pointing to various features on the transparencies and examining a variety of labels. Let students attach arrows to the bulletin board display, pointing to various aspects of label information.

Explain the worksheets and then let the students complete them. Conclude the activity by leading a discussion about the value of information found on labels.

Here are the answers to the worksheets:

Spaghetti Dinner
1. spaghetti
2. 37g
3. onions
4. about 45 cents, $2.67
5. 2

6. Vitamin C
7. No. It gives only 15%.
8. Answers might include net weight, company name and address, grams and percentages of ingredients.
9. circles

Label Lingo

1. Hearty Morning, Hearty Morning
2. Wheat makes up the greatest part of Wheaty Bran. Oat flour makes up the greatest part of Hearty Morning.
3. Answers might include BHT, iron, calcium, copper, zinc, and others.
4. Wheaty Bran: 190
                30
   Hearty Morning: 190
                29
5. Wheaty Bran: about 8 cents; Hearty Morning: about 12 cents.
6. Answers will vary, but students should give answers that reflect their understanding of the importance of label information.

Evaluating the Activity: Did students contribute to the discussion? Did they complete the worksheet accurately? Do students understand the value of the information found on labels?

Extending the Activity: Ask students to bring in two boxes or can labels for similar products (e.g., two cereals, two canned vegetables). Let them work in small groups to compare the products in terms of criteria such as calories per serving, nutritional values, cost per serving, and quantities of salt, sugar, and preservatives. Challenge students to design attractive, informative labels for fictitious food products that they invent.

From *Exploring Mathematics: Activities for Concept and Skill Development,* Copyright © 1990 Scott, Foresman and Company.

$$\div \times - + - \times \div$$

CHAPTER

3

TEACHING AIDS

Mystery Message #1

Replace each letter by a number. Identical letters must be replaced by the same number.

```
    Y
    Y
  + Y
  ─────
   M Y
```

Mystery Message #2

Replace each letter by a number. Identical letters must be replaced by the same number.

```
    O N
    O N
    O N
  + O N
  ───────
    G O
```

Mystery Message #3

Replace each letter by a number. Identical letters must be replaced by the same number.

```
    M A
  +  A
  ─────
    A M
```

Mystery Message #4

Replace each letter by a number. Identical letters must be replaced by the same number.

```
      X
      X
      X
  +   B
  ───────
  B A A A
```

Task Cards for the Puzzle Corner   Teaching Aid 3.1a

From Exploring Mathematics: Activities for Concept and Skill Development, Copyright © 1990 Scott, Foresman and Company.

Mystery Message #5

Replace each letter by a number. Identical letters must be replaced by the same number. The same number cannot be used for more than one letter.

$$
\begin{array}{r}
S E N D \\
+ M O R E \\
\hline
M O N E Y
\end{array}
$$

Mystery Message #6

Replace each letter by a number. Identical letters must be replaced by the same number. The same number cannot be used for more than one letter.

$$
\begin{array}{r}
T H I S \\
I S \\
V E R Y \\
\hline
E A S Y
\end{array}
$$

Mystery Message #7

Replace each letter by a number. Identical letters must be replaced by the same number. The same number cannot be used for more than one letter.

$$
\begin{array}{r}
S P E N D \\
- M O R E \\
\hline
M O N E Y
\end{array}
$$

Mystery Message #8

Replace each letter by a number. Identical letters must be replaced by the same number. The same number cannot be used for more than one letter.

$$
\begin{array}{r}
S A N T A \\
- C L A U S \\
\hline
X M A S
\end{array}
$$

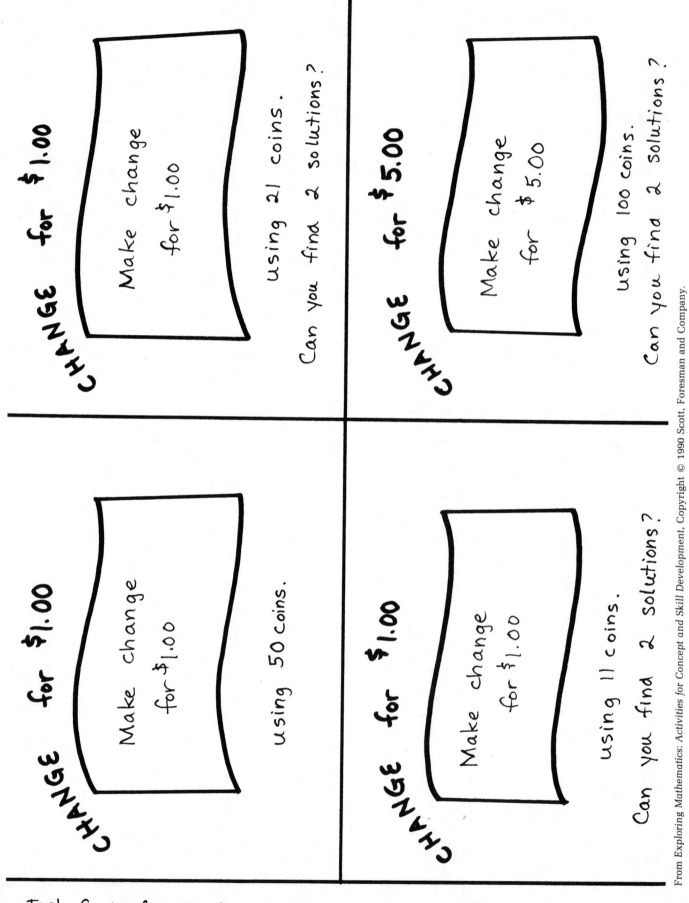

CHANGE for $1.00

Make change
for $1.00

using 50 coins.

CHANGE for $1.00

Make change
for $1.00

using 11 coins.

Can you find 2 solutions?

CHANGE for $1.00

Make change
for $1.00

using 21 coins.

Can you find 2 solutions?

CHANGE for $5.00

Make change
for $5.00

using 100 coins.

Can you find 2 solutions?

Task Cards for the Puzzle Corner

Teaching Aid 3.1c

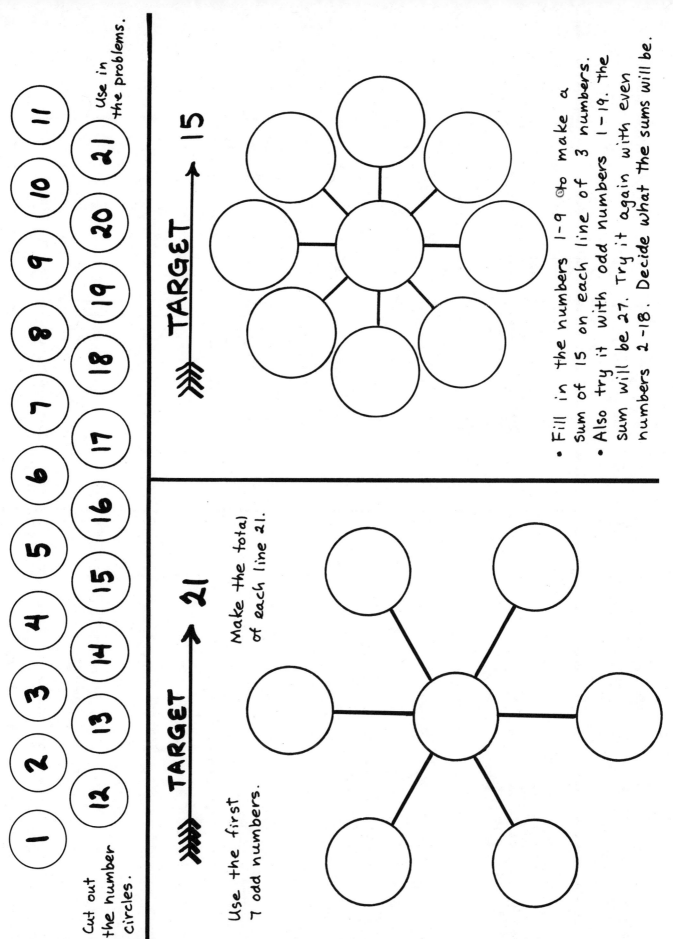

Cut out
the number
circles.

Use in
the problems.

TARGET → 15

TARGET → 21

Use the first
7 odd numbers.

Make the total
of each line 21.

• Fill in the numbers 1–9 to make a
  sum of 15 on each line of 3 numbers.
• Also try it with odd numbers 1–19. The
  sum will be 27. Try it again with even
  numbers 2–18. Decide what the sums will be.

Puzzle Corner Task Cards

Teaching Aid 3.1d

30

TARGET TOTAL

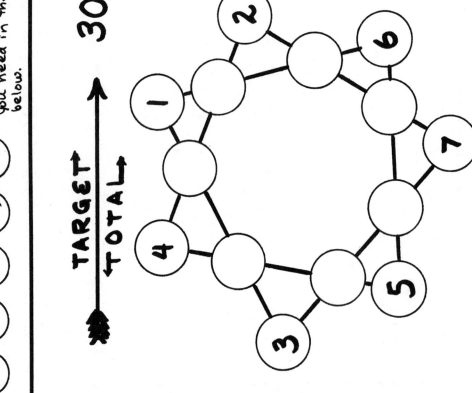

Place 8, 9, 10, 11, 12, 13, and 14 on the empty circles to make a total of 30 on each line of 4 numbers.

26

TARGET TOTAL

Place 2, 3, 4, 7, 9, 10, 11, and 12 on the empty circles to make a total of 26 on each line of 4 numbers.

Teaching Aid 3.1e

SCRAMBLED Sticks #1

Arrange 12 toothpicks like the picture. Now rearrange 3 toothpicks to leave 3 squares.

SCRAMBLED Sticks #2

An equilateral triangle is the same on all sides. It looks like this:

Use 6 toothpicks. From the toothpicks, make 4 equilateral triangles, all the same size.

Rearranging CIRCLES

Arrange 6 pennies or circles like this. Move just 1 circle to make 4 circles in each row -- horizontally and vertically.

SCRAMBLED Sticks #3

When does 5+6 make 9? Let's find out. Arrange 6 toothpicks like this:

| | | | | |

Now add 5 more toothpicks to make nine.

· CURIOUS CUBES ·

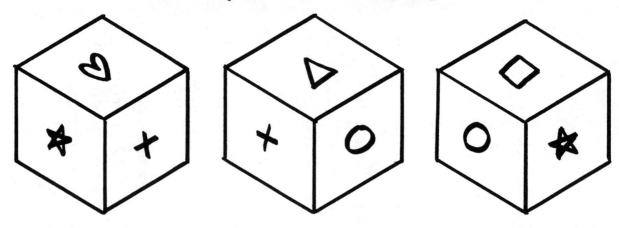

Here are 3 different views of the same cube. The 6 faces are marked with a heart, star, triangle, cross, square, and circle.
- Which picture is opposite the cross?
- Which picture is opposite the circle?
- Which picture is opposite the star?

· CURIOUS CUBES ·

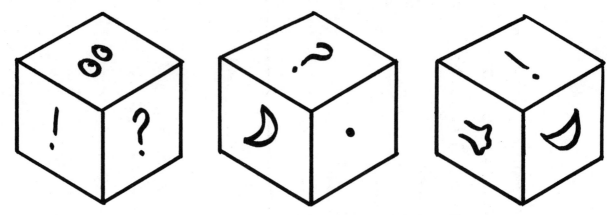

Here are 3 different views of the same cube. The 6 faces are marked with a question mark, period, exclamation point, eyes, nose, and mouth.
- Which picture is opposite the mouth?
- Which picture is opposite the exclamation point?
- Which picture is opposite the question mark?

Task Cards for the Puzzle Corner   Teaching Aid 3.1g

ANSWERS for the Puzzle Corner

Duplicate answers and glue them to answer cards or to the back of the puzzle cards

Mystery Message #1

$$\begin{array}{r} 5 \\ 5 \\ +5 \\ \hline 15 \end{array}$$

Mystery Message #2

$$\begin{array}{r} 23 \\ 23 \\ 23 \\ +23 \\ \hline 92 \end{array} \quad \text{or} \quad \begin{array}{r} 05 \\ 05 \\ 05 \\ +05 \\ \hline 20 \end{array}$$

Mystery Message #3

$$\begin{array}{r} 89 \\ +9 \\ \hline 98 \end{array}$$

Mystery Message #4

$$\begin{array}{r} 999 \\ +1 \\ \hline 1000 \end{array}$$

Mystery Message #5

$$\begin{array}{r} 9567 \\ +1085 \\ \hline 10652 \end{array}$$

Mystery Message #6

3915
15
4826
8756 is one solution

Mystery Message #7

$$\begin{array}{r} 70839 \\ -6458 \\ \hline 64381 \end{array}$$

Mystery Message #8

$$\begin{array}{r} 36156 \\ -28693 \\ \hline 7463 \end{array} \quad \text{or} \quad \begin{array}{r} 24794 \\ -16452 \\ \hline 8342 \end{array}$$

Change for $1.00 – 50 coins

40 – 1¢
8 – 5¢
2 – 10¢

Change for $1.00 – 21 coins

1 – 50¢	2 – 25¢	7 – 10¢
2 – 10¢ or	3 – 10¢ or	4 – 5¢
3 – 5¢	1 – 5¢	10 – 1¢
15 – 1¢	15 – 1¢	

Change for $1.00 – 11 coins

2 – 5¢   3 – 25¢
9 – 10¢ or   1 – 10¢
                    2 – 5¢
                    5 – 1¢

Change for $5.00 – 100 coins

100 – 5¢ or 60 – 1¢
                    39 – 10¢
                    1 – 50¢

Target 21

Target 15

odds

evens

Target 26

Target 30

Sticks #1

Sticks #2

Make a 3-D shape.

Sticks #3

NINE

Circles

Put 1 penny on top of the corner penny.

Curious Cubes

+ – □
O – ♡
★ – △

Curious Cubes

▽ – ◯◯
! – •
? – ₰

Answers to the Puzzle Corner   Teaching Aid 3.2

2, 3, 4, 5

Use only 2, 3, 4, and 5 and any signs you wish to express each number.

1	21
2	22
3	23
4	24
5	25
6	
7	
8	
9	26. Write any numbers you
10	wish here. Just use 2, 3,
11	4, and 5 and any signs
12	and see what results.
13	
14	
15	
16	
17	
18	
19	
20	

teaching Aid 3.3

CALENDAR Cut Ups...

Cut apart the numbers from several calendar pages. Cut apart the task cards too. Arrange the numbers face down in the center of your workspace. Choose task cards. Take turns working the tasks and checking each other. Do as much of the computation as possible in your head.

Teaching Aid 3.4a

Select 3 numbers.
Multiply the large two.
Subtract the smaller value.

8   7   1

$18 \times 7 = 126$

$126 - 1 = 125$

Pick 4 numbers.
Add them.
Divide the sum by 6.

2   7   15   28

$2 + 7 + 15 + 28 = 52$

$52 \div 6 = 8 \, r \, 4$

Choose 5 numbers.
Find their average value.

4   8   12   25   36

$4 + 8 + 12 + 25 + 36 = 79$

$79 \div 5 = 15 \frac{4}{5}$

Select 6 numbers.
Make 2 larger numbers from them.
Subtract the smaller from the larger number.

   6   21   3
− 5   4   8
_____
   5   6   6   5

Pick 3 numbers.
Arrange them to make the largest possible number.

9   12   19

9 19 12

"91912"

Choose 3 numbers.
Multiply them.

13   2   7

$13 \times 2 \times 7 = 182$

Choose 4 numbers.
Arrange them to make the smallest possible value. Read the number.

14   2   30   9

9   30   2   14

"one hundred forty-two thousand, 3 hundred nine"

Make up and work your own "Calendar Cut Up" activity.

CALENDAR MAGIC!

BLOCK O' NINE

1. Choose a block of 9 calendar days
2. Circle any number in the first row. Cross out the other numbers in the same row and column.
3. Circle either of the remaining numbers in the second row. Cross out the other numbers in the same row and column.
4. Circle the remaining number.
5. Now the magic! Compare the sum of the 3 circled numbers to the center number. What do you find?

LIGHTNING ADDITION

1. Find the sum of all the numbers in a week. Multiply 7 times the first number. Add 21. Try it out for several different full (7 day) weeks.
2. Find the sum of the numbers in any 2 full weeks. Multiply 14 times the value of the first day in the block. Add 91. Check it out.
3. Why do these "Lightning Addition" tricks work?

SUMS ALL AROUND

1. Look at the 8 numerals that surround another numeral on the calendar. Use 21 for example.
2. The sum of the numbers in each row, column, and diagonal that passes through 21 is special. Why?
3. Add up the right and left columns. What happens this time?
4. Add all the numbers in the top and bottom rows. What happens here?
5. Try the steps with other numbers in the center. See what happens.

```
        1  2  3
 4  5  6  7  8  9  10
11 12 13 14 15 16 17
18 19 20 21 22 23 24
25 26 27 28 29 30
```

13 + 14 + 15 + 27 +
28 + 29 = ?

MORE CALENDAR SUMS

1. For any month, choose a square of 16 days.
2. Circle any number in the first row. Cross out all numbers below it.
3. Circle any number that is left in the second row. Cross out the numbers above and below it.
4. Circle a number that is left in the third row. Cross out numbers above and below it.
5. Circle the remaining number in the fourth row.
6. Add the circled numbers. Add the 4 corner numbers. What do you find?

```
        1  2
 3  4  5  6  7  8  9
10 11 12 13 14 15 16
17 18 19 20 21 22 23
24 25 26 27 28 29 30
```

7 + 12 + 20 + 29 = ?
5 + 8 + 26 + 17 = ?

NUMBER CLUES

1. • I'm a multiple of 5.
   • I'm odd.
   • When you double me, then add 10, you get 100.
   • Who am I?

2. • I'm a perfect square.
   • the sum of my digits is 10.
   • I'm less than 100.
   • Who am I?

3. • I'm a 3-digit number.
   • Each of my digits is odd.
   • My ones and tens digit are the same. Their sum is 2.
   • My hundreds digit is more than 1 but less than 5.
   • Who am I?

4. • I'm less than 100.
   • I'm divisible by 2, 4, and 21.
   • My tens digit is twice the value of my ones digit.
   • Who am I?

5. • I'm a prime number.
   • I'm more than 70 but less than 90.
   • the sum of my digits is 16.
   • Who am I?

6. • I'm greater than 100 but less than 200.
   • I'm divisible by lots of numbers -- 1, 2, 3, 4, 5, 6, 8, 12, 15, and 20.
   • the sum of my digits is only 3.
   • Who am I?

7. • I'm less than 1000 but more than 100.
   • the sum of my digits is 13.
   • My hundreds digit is 3 times my tens digit.
   • My ones digit is 3 more than my tens digit.
   • Who am I?

USE THE CLUES...
FIND THE MYSTERY NUMBERS

Teaching Aid 3.5

SPAGHETTI DINNER

Nutritional Information

Serving size	156g
Calories	210
Protein	7g
Carbohydrates	37g
Fat	8g

USA RDA Requirement of Daily Allowances

protein	10%	vitamin C	15%
iron	14%	niacin	6%

Ingredients: Spaghetti, tomatoes, onions, peppers, beef, cornstarch, wheat flour, preservatives, spices

HEARTY EATERS

Chicago, Illinois 60655

Directions: Pour into a pan. Heat until simmering. 2 servings

51 000 2958

HEARTY ♥ EATERS

BRAND

SPAGHETTI
with
Tomatoes & Beef

Net. Wt. 11 oz. 312g

Study the picture of the label. Answer the questions.

1. Which ingredient is used most in the spaghetti?
2. How many grams of carbohydrate are in each serving?
3. What ingredient is listed third?
4. If a can of spaghetti costs 89¢, what is the cost of a serving? Of 6 servings?
5. How many servings does 1 can make?
6. this product gives you the largest RDA percentage of which nutrient?
7. Does the spaghetti give you all the vitamin C you need in a day? How can you tell?
8. List some other things the label tells you.
9. Cut out the label and curve it around like a can. What do the tops and bottoms look like?

Teaching Aid 3.6a

From Exploring Mathematics: Activities for Concept and Skill Development, Copyright © 1990 Scott, Foresman and Company.

LABEL LINGO

Study the nutrition information from the pictures of side panels of cereal boxes. Answer the questions.

1. Which cereal has more sugar?   salt?

2. Which ingredient makes up the greatest part of each cereal?

3. What are some added minerals and preservatives for each cereal?

4. Fill in the chart:

Cereal		
Calories with milk		
Grams Carbohydrate with milk		

5. If Wheaty Bran costs $1.94 and Hearty Morning costs $1.69, what is the cost of each per serving?

6. Which cereal would you buy? Why?

All Natural WHEATY BRAN

Nutrition Information per serving

Serving size   ⅔ cup
(1oz., 28g)

Servings per box   24

Wheaty Bran	1oz.	with ¼ c. milk
Calories	110	190
Protein	3g	7g
Carbohydrate	24g	30g
Fat	1g	5g
Sodium	0 mg	60mg

Percentage of U.S.R. Daily Allowances

Natural Wheaty Bran	1oz.	with ¼ c. milk
Protein	4	15
Vitamin A	*	2
Vitamin C	*	*
Thiamine	4	8
Riboflavin	*	12
Niacin	8	8
Calcium	*	15
Iron	6	6
Phosphorus	10	20
Magnesium	8	10
Zinc	4	8
Copper	6	8

* Less than 2% of USRDA of this nutrient.

Ingredients: 100% natural whole wheat. To preserve the natural flavor, BHT is added to packaging material.

Natural Cereals, Inc.
Cedar Rapids, Iowa

Hearty Morning ♥ Wheat Cereal

NUTRITION INFORMATION per SERVING

Serving Size ... 1oz (28g)

Servings per package 14

	1oz Hearty Morning	Hearty Morning, ¼c. milk
CALORIES	110	190
PROTEIN	3g	7g
CARBOHYDRATE	23g	29g
FAT	1g	5g
SODIUM	255mg	315mg

Percentages of USRDA Allowances

PROTEIN	4	25
VITAMIN A	25	30
VITAMIN C	25	25
THIAMINE	25	30
RIBOFLAVIN	25	35
NIACIN	25	25
CALCIUM	2	15
IRON	25	25
VITAMIN D	10	25
VITAMIN B₆	25	30
PHOSPHORUS	25	35
MAGNESIUM	10	20
ZINC	4	6
COPPER	6	6

Ingredients: oat flour, sugar, wheat germ, wheat starch, honey, brown sugar, almonds, trisodium phosphate, sodium ascorb, calcium carbonate, iron, vitamin A, vitamin B₁₂.

Teaching Aid 3.6b

Bulletin Board Ideas...

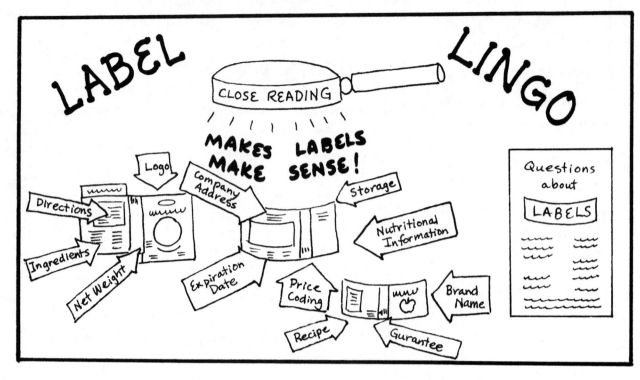

Display real can labels and flattened boxes on the bulletin board. Question children about pertinent information and let them place the arrows labeling each part on the bulletin board. Add more arrows to label other pertinent information. Encourage children to add questions to the list. You might start with questions such as these:

Take a close look at the labels and try to answer these questions:

1. What ingredient makes up the largest proportion of _____ (product)?

2. What does US RDA mean?

3. Does _____ contain half of the recommended daily allowance for carbohydrates?

4. If you were dissatisfied with _____ (product), and wanted to write to its manufacturer, where would you find its address?

5. Does _____ contain a large proportion of fat? How do you know?

6. How should _____ be stored?

7. Which label do you find the most attractive? Why?

8. How many grams of protein does _____ contain in a serving?

9. Would the recipe on _____ make you want to buy the product? Why?

10. How do you cook _____ in a microwave oven? How does the microwaving time compare to the stove-top cooking time?

Teaching Aid 3.6c

From Exploring Mathematics: Activities for Concept and Skill Development, Copyright © 1990 Scott, Foresman and Company.

4
Minds and Tools Working Together: Calculators

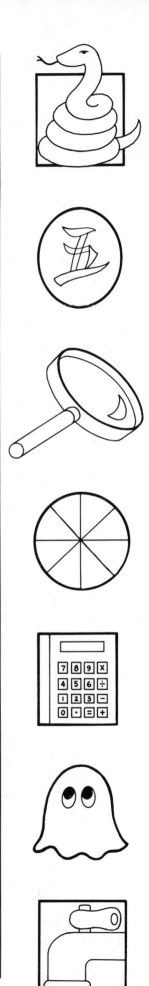

Calculators are mathematical tools designed to be used intelligently, not devices for mindless button pushing. Calculators don't replace skillful estimating, knowledge of basic facts, or sensible selection of mathematical operations. Rather, they are tools for rapid calculation of problems in which the numbers are too large to work with mentally. As they use calculators, students should develop habits of thinking before keying in numbers and operations, and they should always check answers to make sure that the results shown on the calculator are reasonable.

The problems and activities in this chapter encourage students to use calculators in a variety of ways. By calling for various problem-solving skills, moreover, the activities encourage students to use their minds and develop their repertoire of heuristic techniques. Many of the activities also feature creative aspects and opportunities for students to share their thoughts about problems with others.

In classrooms where there is not a sufficient number of calculators for each student to use one independently, the activities can be worked in groups or in a learning center.

CALCULATING CROSSTICS

To implement the connection between thinking and using an electronic tool, students use their calculators only to do those computations they can't do mentally.

Objectives: Students will work problems mentally or on calculators and fill in the answers on a crosstic form. They will work with place value, powers of 10 and other numbers, and subtraction involving many zeroes.

Materials: Paper to duplicate worksheets from Teaching Aids 4.1a and b, a calculator for each group of two or three students who do not have their own.

Preparing for the Activity: Duplicate copies of the crosstic sheets.

Conducting the Activity: Emphasize to the students that they should do as much of each problem as possible in their heads. Tell them to look over each problem before using the calculator in order to see what solving strategies they might use.

Most students will want to work the problems first and then see where the answers fit in the crosstic blanks. Let the students work the crosstics, check their answers, and then discuss the various strategies they used in working the problems.

Here are the answers to the worksheet crosstics:

4.1a

4.1b

Evaluating the Activity: Students can check their own papers. Listen to their discussion of strategies and ways to find answers.

From *Exploring Mathematics: Activities for Concept and Skill Development*, Copyright © 1990 Scott, Foresman and Company.

Extending the Activity: Make other crosstics based on those skills your students need to practice. Encourage interested students to create crosstics for their classmates.

CALORIE COUNTERS

Even in the intermediate grades, students are interested in calories. Problems that involve calorie counts encourage estimating and figuring totals.

Objectives: Students will choose foods, estimate numbers of calories, and figure total numbers of calories. While working the problems, students will read a calorie chart.

Materials: Paper to duplicate a copy of the calorie chart (Teaching Aid 4.2a) and task cards (Teaching Aid 4.2b) for each group of three or four students, scissors, a calculator for each group of students who do not have their own.

Preparing for the Activity: Duplicate calorie charts and task cards.

Conducting the Activity: Organize students into groups of three or four. Have each group cut their task cards apart and then work on the problems. Since answers will vary based on the students' food choices, one or two students can work the problems and let the others check them. Let groups exchange their "make a problem" cards and then check each other's solutions.

Evaluating the Activity: Spot-check the students' work to see that they select foods from the specified groups, use the chart correctly, and calculate the totals accurately. Observe whether group members work cooperatively.

Extending the Activity: Encourage students to create additional calorie problems for each other. Perhaps they could research the numbers of calories that a person uses when doing certain physical activities and then choose foods whose calorie values offset the calories used up. Have students glue pictures of foods they like to paper plates, figure the number of calories in the foods they selected, and display the plates and calorie values on a bulletin board.

CALCULATORS VERSUS THINKERS

This game, pitting "thinkers" against classmates equipped with calculators, illustrates the strengths and limitations of both "people power" and calculator power.

Objectives: Children will take turns responding to problems given orally, working the problems either in their heads or on calculators.

Materials: Several calculators.

Preparing for the Activity: Assemble a list of problems and answers.

Conducting the Activity: Divide your class into two fairly evenly matched teams, and choose two children to help you in conducting the contest. Designate one team the "calculators" and the other the "thinkers"; provide a calculator to each three or four children on the calculator team.

Announce the rules for the game. You will say each problem once. "Calculators" must punch the problem into their calculators, get an answer, and hold up their calculators to show that they are finished. "Thinkers" may write down the problems or do them entirely in their heads as they choose, but they must write legible answers and then raise their hands to indicate that they are finished. The first child to get the right answer receives five points; other team members who solve the problem correctly receive one point.

Designate three contestants from both teams to work on each problem. Call out the problem, and have your helpers watch to see who finishes first. Check answers and assign points for correct answers. Vary the problems—using some with basic facts and others involving multi-digit computations. The "thinkers" will tend to finish first with the basic fact problems. The "calculators" will probably finish first with the problems involving multi-digit computations, as long as they enter the numbers accurately. Play several rounds; then let your "thinkers" change places with the "calculators" and work several more problems.

Discuss with the children the fact that most people can work simple problems in their heads very quickly. When problems are longer, however, the calculator's speed and accuracy provide a distinct advantage. Encourage the children to talk about the need to enter numbers into the calculator accurately.

Conduct "Calculators Versus Thinkers" contests once or twice a month. Once students understand the rules, the contests themselves take just 10 to 15 minutes of class time. You might even keep a running score of team performance.

Evaluating the Activity: Note which children use the calculators quickly and accurately and which children need help and guidance. Assess the children's ability to work problems mentally and at the chalkboard.

From Exploring Mathematics: Activities for Concept and Skill Development, Copyright © 1990 Scott, Foresman and Company.

Extending the Activity: Ask the children for suggestions regarding different competitions in which they might use calculators. Let groups of children play "Calculators Versus Thinkers" on their own.

+ ÷ ✕ − + − ✕ ÷ +

PERSONALIZED PROBLEMS

These problems spark interest because they are based on data that varies with each student. Although some of the problems involve extensive computation, use of calculators makes the computation easy!

Objectives: Students will measure to get personal data. Students will solve problems with the aid of calculators.

Materials: Paper to duplicate task cards from Teaching Aid 4.3a and b, calculators, measuring equipment (measuring tapes, watch with a second hand, meter stick or trundle wheel).

Preparing for the Activity: Gather measuring equipment and duplicate the task cards.

Conducting the Activity: Organize students into groups of three or four. Assign a problem to each group, or let each group choose a problem. Have each group determine its own procedure for working the problem, and then let the various groups figure and agree on one answer for all group members. Share answers, and let each group explain its problem-solving strategies.

Both answers and strategies will vary because of the nature of the problems. One strategy for solving each problem is described below, but other ways of solving the problems are possible.

Walkin' On. Divide the time for 30m by your time in seconds. This will give your speed in meters per second. Divide 1000 by your speed to get your speed for 1000m.

How Many Breaths? One way to work it out is breaths per minute multiplied by 60 (minutes per hour) multiplied by 24 (hours per day). Then figure the days you have lived (your age in years multiplied by 365.25, plus the number of days since your last birthday) multiplied by your number of breaths per day. Finally, count the number of days between now and Christmas, multiply this number by your breaths per day, and add on the number of breaths for the rest of today.

How Old Are You? In days: Multiply your number of years by 365.25 and add on the number of days since your last birthday. In minutes: Multiply your first answer by 24 (hours in a day) and then by 60 (minutes in an hour). Add on 60 times the number of hours you've lived today. In seconds: Multiply the minute answer by 60.

Use Your Height (4.3a). Multiply 1000 by 100 to get the number of cm in one km. Now divide by your height. For the New York to Los Angeles measurement, multiply 4450 by 100, and then divide by your height.

Use Your Pulse Rate. Figure your pulse per minute and multiply by 60 (minutes per hour) and then by 24 (hours in a day). To find the approximate number of times your heart will beat by age 40, multiply your number of beats per day by 365.25. Now multiply by 40.

Arm Spans. Measure the perimeter of the room in meters. Multiply by 100 to get the number of centimeters. Divide this figure by your arm span. For the measurement to the moon, multiply 384 000 km by 1000 and then by 100 to get the number of cm to the moon. Then divide that figure by your arm span.

Around Your Wrist. Measure your waist in cm. Now divide your waist measurement by your wrist measurement. For the second measurement, divide your wrist measurement by your little finger measurement. Finally, divide your height by your wrist measurement.

Use Your Height (4.3b). Multiply 140m by 100 to get the number of cm in the height of the World Trade Center. Divide this figure by your height in cm. For the second problem, multiply 14m by 100 to get the number of cm in the dinosaur's height; then divide by your height.

Evaluating the Activity: Assess the process and results: Did group members work cooperatively and productively? Did they share results in a way that their classmates could understand? Did students use measuring tools and calculators accurately and efficiently?

Extending the Activity: Put the task cards in a learning center for small group or individual use. Let students create and solve similar problems. Challenge a computer whiz to figure the answer to a personalized problem once a user enters personal data.

From Exploring Mathematics: Activities for Concept and Skill Development, Copyright © 1990 Scott, Foresman and Company.

MYSTERY MESSAGES

Students gain lots of computation practice as they work out mystery messages.

Objectives: Students will work computations and use a code to produce a message.

Materials: Paper to duplicate worksheet from Teaching Aid 4.4, calculators.

Preparing for the Activity: Duplicate a "Mystery Message" worksheet for each student.

Conducting the Activity: Show students how to work the problems in their heads or on paper, then select letters for each answer from the code. Tell them that when they fill in the letters on the worksheet they will see a mystery message.
   Here are the answers to the mystery messages:

   Message #1: Tennis the sum of five and five.
   Message #2: Dozen anyone live here anymore?

Evaluating the Activity: Check the children's worksheets by glancing at the message.

Extending the Activity: Encourage interested students to create messages for their classmates. Make other messages based on the students' current interests or seasonal events.

CHAPTER 4

4

TEACHING AIDS

CALCULATING CROSTIC

Fill in the crostic form. Find answers to the problems below. Do as much work as you can in your head. Work the remaining problems on a calculator.

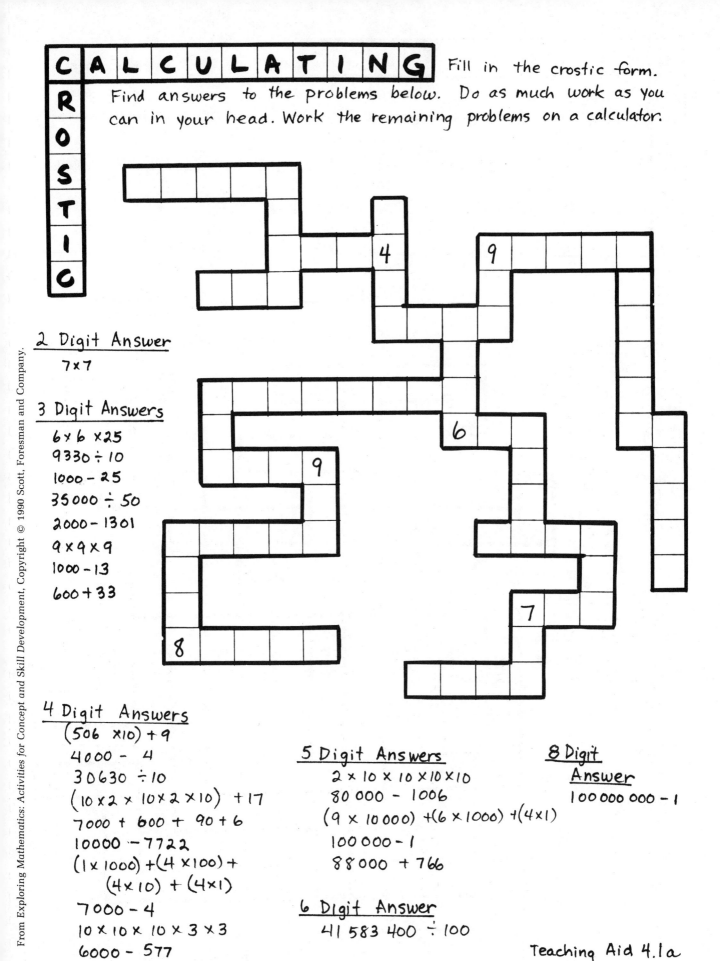

2 Digit Answer
7 × 7

3 Digit Answers
6 × 6 × 25
9330 ÷ 10
1000 − 25
35000 ÷ 50
2000 − 1301
9 × 9 × 9
1000 − 13
600 + 33

4 Digit Answers
(506 × 10) + 9
4000 − 4
30630 ÷ 10
(10 × 2 × 10 × 2 × 10) + 17
7000 + 600 + 90 + 6
10000 − 7722
(1 × 1000) + (4 × 100) +
   (4 × 10) + (4 × 1)
7000 − 4
10 × 10 × 10 × 3 × 3
6000 − 577

5 Digit Answers
2 × 10 × 10 × 10 × 10
80 000 − 1006
(9 × 10 000) + (6 × 1000) + (4 × 1)
100 000 − 1
88 000 + 766

6 Digit Answer
41 583 400 ÷ 100

8 Digit Answer
100 000 000 − 1

Teaching Aid 4.1a

CROSTIC

C A L C U L A T I N G

Fill in the crostic form with answers to the problems below. Do as much work as you can in your head. Work the remaining problems on a calculator.

2 Digit Answers
20 − 4
(10 × 10) − 16
2 × 2 × 2 × 2 × 2
(10 × 10) − 1
Half of 178

3 Digit Answers
91 200 ÷ 100
8 × 8 × 10
19 × 19
25 × 25
11 × 11
21 × 21

4 Digit Answers
8 × 8 × 8 × 8
(10 × 10 × 10) + 266
9966 ÷ 3
8 × 8 × 10 × 10
13 × 13 × 10
204 × 10
11 × 10 × 11

5 Digit Answers
3 (10000 + 1000 + 10 + 1)
100 000 − 77 778
43 201 × 2
(3 × 3 × 3 × 1000) + 3
40 000 + 4000 + 400 + 44
4 (10 000 + 2000 + 300 + 40 + 5)

6 Digit Answers
1 000 000 − 12
18 × 18 × 10 × 10 × 10
9 × 10 × 11 × 10 × 100
(566 × 1000) ÷ 2
792 904 ÷ 2

7 Digit Answers
3 × 3 × 1000 × 1000
1100 × 1100

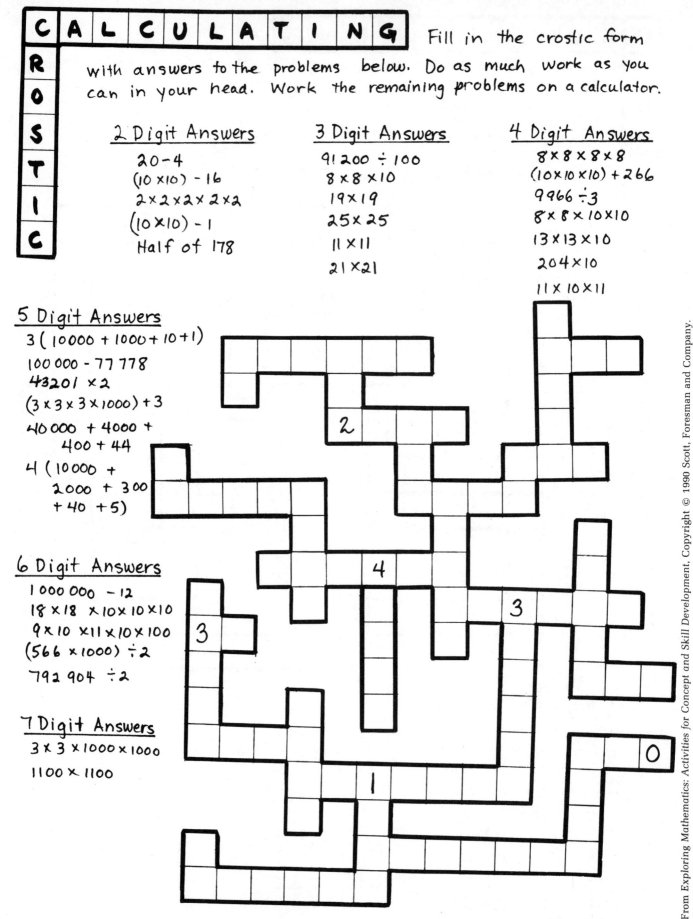

Teaching Aid 4.1b

From Exploring Mathematics: Activities for Concept and Skill Development, Copyright © 1990 Scott, Foresman and Company.

CALORIE Chart

Fruits and Vegetables

Banana - 1 medium	85
Blueberries - 250ml (1c)	85
Beans, baked - 250ml	325
Beans, green - 250ml	25
Carrots - 250ml	25
Coleslaw - 250ml	102
Apple - 1 medium	120
Lettuce - 4 leaves	10
Orange - 1 medium	120
Orange juice - 250ml	100
Peach - medium	35
Spinach - 500ml	20
Tomato - 1 medium	30

Milk Products

Butter - 15ml (1T.)	100
Cheese - 28g. (1oz.)	115
Cocoa - 28g (1oz.)	235
Ice Cream - 1 scoop	175
Milk	
whole - 250ml (1c.)	165
chocolate - 250ml	190
low fat - 250ml	120
Milk shake - 300ml (10oz.)	400
Yogurt	
plain	120
fruit	220
Whipped cream - 15ml	25

Breads and Cereals

Bread, - 1 slice	70
raisin bread	80
Bagel - 1 medium	125
Biscuit - 1 medium	130
Cereal - 250ml (1c.)	
cornflakes	120
sugar cereal	150
Cinnamon roll - 1med.	160
Cornbread - 1 square	150
Crackers - 2 square	40
Donut - 1 medium	150
Muffin - 1 medium	120
Pancake - 2 medium	220
Waffle - 1 medium	250

Meats

Bacon - 2 slices	95
Bologna - 28g (1oz.)	115
Chicken - 85g (3oz.)	
broiled	115
fried	200
Chili with beans - 250ml	300
Fish, fried - 85g	250
Ham - 85g	340
Hamburger - 85g	250
Hot dog - 60g (2oz.)	175
Peanut butter - 15ml (1T.)	100
Roast beef - 85g	150
Tuna fish - 85g	170
Sausage - 1 medium patty	190

Extras

Chocolate cake - 1 slice	260
Cookies - 1 medium	
Brownie	120
Sugar cookie	60
Chocolate bar - 28g (1oz.)	160
Jam - 15ml (1T.)	50
Peanut candy bar	150
Pie - 1 slice	300
Salad dressing - 15ml	100
Soft drink - 250ml (1c.)	110

A MEAL

Select foods for a meal including something from the meat group, milk group, bread and cereals group, and fruit and vegetable group. Guess how many calories your meal will include. Calculate the actual calories from the chart.

A SNACK

Choose one snack food and a beverage. Estimate the number of calories you would eat. Use the chart to find and calculate the actual number of calories in your snack.

1000 CALORIES

Choose some things you would like to eat. Try to keep your total close to 1000 calories. Check yourself by using the chart and calculating the total.

A SANDWICH!

Build a "dagwood sandwich." Choose at least 5 ingredients. How many calories do you guess your sandwich will contain? Calculate the actual number.

A PICNIC

Choose at least 5 foods for a picnic. Try to estimate the total number of calories in all your picnic foods. Now use the chart and your calculator to check out the total number of calories.

CALORIES FOR A DAY

Target a daily total of calories. Plan 3 meals and 1 or 2 snacks. Add up the calories you would consume. How close were you to your target number?

BIG BREAKFAST

Plan a hearty breakfast to eat on a day when you're not too rushed. Include foods from at least 3 different food groups. Estimate your total calories. Calculate the actual total.

MAKE A PROBLEM

Write a calorie problem for a classmate.

Calorie Counters Task Cards   Teaching Aid 4.2b

From Exploring Mathematics: Activities for Concept and Skill Development, Copyright © 1990 Scott, Foresman and Company.

HOW MANY BREATHS?

puff
puff

Time your breathing for 3 or 4 minutes, then figure your average breaths per minute. Use a calculator to help you figure:

- the number of breaths you take each day.
- the number of breaths you've taken so far in your life.
- the number of breaths you'll take between now and Christmas.

USE YOUR HEIGHT

Measure your height in centimeters. With the help of your calculator, figure out:

- How many of "your heights" make 1 kilometer?
- How many of "your heights" stretch from New York to Los Angeles (4450 km)?

WALKIN' ON...

Time yourself in seconds as you walk over a 30 meter course. Figure your average speed in meters/second. Now figure how long it would take you to walk 1 kilometer (1000 m) at the same speed you walked on the 30 m course.

How OLD Are You?

- In days?
- In minutes?
- In seconds?

Use a calculator to help you figure your age!

Teaching Aid 4.3a

ARM SPANS

Stand with your arms and fingers outstretched. Measure your armspan in centimeters. Now calculate:

- The number of armspans to reach around your classroom.

- The number of armspans between Earth and the moon! (About 384 000 kilometers)

USE YOUR HEIGHT

Use your height (measured in centimeters) and figure:

- The number of "your heights" needed to reach the top of the World Trade Center in New York (140m).

- The number of "your heights" needed to equal tyrannosaurus rex's height (14m).

USE YOUR PULSE RATE

Take your pulse for 3 or 4 minutes. Find your average number of heart beats per minute. Now use this rate -- and your calculator -- to help you figure:

- The number of times your heart beats in a day.

- The approximate number of times your heart has beaten from birth to age 40.

Around Your WRIST

Measure around your wrist in centimeters using a tape measure. Now figure these with a calculator:

- Your waist is how many times larger than your wrist?

- Your wrist is how many times the circumference of your little finger?

- Your height is how many times your wrist?

Personalized Problems   Task Cards   Teaching Aid 4.3 b

MYSTERY MESSAGES

Work the problems in your head or with a calculator. Use the code to fill in the letters at the bottom. The letters will form a mystery message -- the answer to a knock-knock joke.

CODE

A - 30	F - 14	K - 22	P - 125	U - 40
B - 100	G - 28	L - 65	Q - 90	V - 600
C - 85	H - 37	M - 15	R - 200	W - 64
D - 62	I - 25	N - 50	S - 45	X - 12
E - 225	J - 300	O - 32	T - 49	Y - 700
				Z - 128

MESSAGE #1

1. 7×7
2. $(2 \times 10 \times 10) + (5 \times 5)$
3. $250 \div 5$
4. $5 \times 2 \times 5$
5. $625 \div 25$
6. $4500 \div 100$
7. $9800 \div 200$
8. $12 + 25$
9. 15×15
10. $3 \times 3 \times 5$
11. $2 \times 2 \times 5 \times 2$
12. $45 \div 3$
13. $2 \times 2 \times 2 \times 2 \times 2$
14. $30 - 16$
15. $28 \div 2$
16. $13 + 12$
17. $2 \times 3 \times 10 \times 10$
18. $22500 \div 100$
19. $2 \times 3 \times 5$
20. $(5 \times 10) + (10 \times 0)$
21. 31×2
22. $100 - 86$
23. $52 - 27$
24. $1004 - 404$
25. $(3 \times 5) \times (3 \times 5)$

" Knock, knock. "
" Who's there? "
" Tennis. "
" Tennis who? "

MESSAGE #2

1. $50 + 12$
2. $100 - 68$
3. $4 \times 4 \times 4 \times 2$
4. $(8 \times 25) + (5 \times 5)$
5. $39 + 11$
6. $737 - 707$
7. $560 - 510$
8. $10 \times 10 \times 7$
9. $17 + 15$
10. $5000 \div 100$
11. $(10 \times 10) + (5 \times 20) + 25$
12. 13×5
13. $(4 \times 5 \times 10) \div (5 + 3)$
14. $60000 \div 100$
15. $300 - 75$
16. $450 - 413$
17. $225000 \div 1000$
18. $2 \times 2 \times 2 \times 5 \times 5$
19. 15×15
20. $12 + 18$
21. $26 + 24$
22. $1028 - 328$
23. $40 - 25$
24. $640 \div 20$
25. $178 + 22$
26. $1000 - 775$

" Knock, knock "
" Who's there? "
" Dozen. "
" Dozen who? "

Message #1 blanks:
1 2 3 4 5 6 7 8 9 10 11 12
13 14 15 16 17 18 19 20 21 22 23 24 25

Message #2 blanks:
1 2 3 4 5 6 7 8 9 10 11 12 13 14 15
16 17 18 19 20 21 22 23 24 25 26 ?

5
Parts and Wholes: Fractions and Decimals

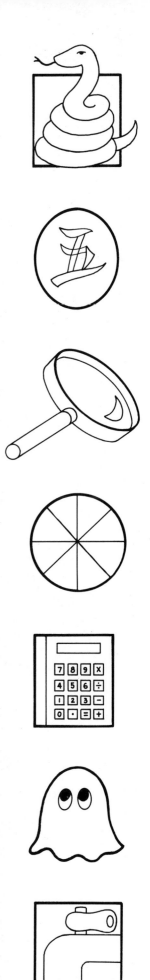

Students need a strong conceptual base for their study of rational numbers. Without a firm understanding of the meanings and relationships of fractions and decimals, work with rational numbers becomes an exercise in memorizing rules or "pushing" decimal points around. Students can gain useful, meaningful concepts of rational numbers by using models of numerical values and relationships. They can develop and retain fraction concepts by working with diagrams, charts, and movable pieces.

Students in the intermediate grades also need opportunities to develop and refine skills in working with fractions. They need practice in figuring equivalent fractions, ordering fractions and decimals, and performing computations in order to do these operations quickly and accurately. Often, students can self-check their practice work or have it checked by classmates.

The activities in this chapter will help students build a firm foundation for subsequent work with rational numbers. In addition to complementing textbook and pencil/paper work, these activities provide opportunities for students to work together, making them especially appealing and motivating to children in grades four through six.

FRACTION BARS

Fraction bars vividly show relationships between fractions and a whole.

Objectives: Students will cut out fraction bars and use the bars to show equivalent fractions, fractional relationships, and operations with fractions.

Materials: Paper to duplicate fraction bars and worksheets from Teaching Aid 5.1, scissors, crayons or markers, glue, transparency (optional), small plastic bags or paper clips.

Preparing for the Activities: Duplicate copies of the fraction bars (Teaching Aid 5.1a) and the worksheets (Teaching Aid 5.1b) for each student. Duplicate a copy of the number cube (Teaching Aid 2.1a) for each group of three or four students. If you wish, you can make a transparency of the fraction bars.

Conducting the Activities: Have the students color their fraction bars according to the following code: whole—red, halves—yellow, fourths—blue, eighths—orange, sixteenths— green. Then tell the students to cut their bars apart carefully.

Allow a few minutes for the students to explore the relative sizes of their bars. Ask them to show relationships—e.g., how many eighths in a whole, how many sixteenths in a fourth. Organize students into groups of four and have them do problems 1, 2, and 3 on the left of the worksheet. Discuss the results, and perhaps use the transparency to show the results to the entire class.

Play a "Make a Whole" game. Give a number cube pattern to each group of four students, and have them number the faces of the cube as follows: $+1/16$, $-1/16$, $+1/16$, $+1/8$, $-1/8$, $+1/4$. Have the students cut out and construct the cube. Each student should then lay out the "whole" piece. To play, the students take turns throwing the cube and arranging fractional parts on top of the whole according to what fraction appears on the top of the cube. They should physically change pieces as required. For example, if a student has $1/8$ and must subtract $1/16$, he or she should exchange the $1/8$ for $1/16$ and $1/16$, then subtract $1/16$. The first student who reaches the whole—or the first group in which each member reaches the whole—wins the game.

Finally, have the students try problems 1–12 on the right of the worksheet. These problems involve operations with fractions. Discuss some results with the entire group. Have the students fasten their fraction bars together with paper clips and store them in their math books or in small plastic bags for subsequent use.

Evaluating the Activities: Circulate around the room as students are working and see who handles and exchanges bars confidently and who needs extra help. Observe who reports answers to the entire group in an understandable way.

From Exploring Mathematics: Activities for Concept and Skill Development, Copyright © 1990 Scott, Foresman and Company.

Extending the Activities: Have students work with the fraction bars to make a whole with the smallest number of pieces. For example, have the students start with 5/8 and then use the smallest number of pieces (e.g., 1/4 or 1/8) they can to make a whole. Or they can start with 1/16 and make a whole with the smallest number of pieces (1/2 + 1/4 + 1/8 + 1/16 + 1/16).

Make problems similar to those on the worksheets, and have students work the problems independently or in groups. Have each student make a set of bars to show halves, thirds, sixths, and twelfths and then use the bars to work problems.

+ ÷ × − + − × ÷ +

FRACTION WHEELS

Fraction wheels are intriguing for students to manipulate. This activity features two different patterns that students can make and use to practice equivalent fractions.

Objectives: Students will make and use fraction wheels to practice equivalent fractions.

Materials: Paper to duplicate fraction wheels from Teaching Aid 5.2a and b, 14 spring-fastener clothespins for the fraction wheel from Teaching Aid 5.2a, fine-line permanent markers, brads, scissors, crayons.

Preparing for the Activity: Duplicate copies of the fraction wheels.

Conducting the Activity: Organize students in groups of three or four and let them make the wheels. For each clothespin wheel, have students use the permanent markers to mark fractions on each side of the clothespins as shown on the pattern. If you wish, you can have students mark answers on the back of the fraction wheels for self-checking.

After they complete the wheels, let students work with their wheels to practice equivalent fractions. Have them check each other or use the answers from the backs of the wheels to check themselves.

Evaluating the Activity: Observe the students and ascertain who works confidently and who needs more help. Assess the students' ability to work cooperatively in groups.

Extending the Activity: Let students use their fraction bars to show equivalent fractions. Have them use wheel patterns with different equivalent fractions or with simple computation problems such as 2 x 1/4 or 7/8 − 1/8.

FRACTION BATTLE

Students make many comparisons of fraction values in a short time as they play this fast-paced game.

Objectives: Students will work in pairs and compare values of fractions.

Materials: Paper to reproduce fraction cards from Teaching Aid 5.3a and b, laminating material.

Preparing for the Activity: Duplicate and laminate the fraction cards. Cut them apart or have the students do so.

Conducting the Activity: Show the students how to play the game according to the following rules. Each pair of students uses a pack of shuffled cards. They deal out all the cards and then turn over their top cards simultaneously. The student with the card having the higher value takes both cards. If the values are equal, the students put the cards aside in a third pile. Students may refer to the answer card, which shows the fractions from smallest to largest, for help in determining fraction values. The player who has the most cards at the end of the game is the winner.

Evaluating the Activity: Observe the students and see if they play cooperatively. Spot-check to see if judgments of card values seem accurate. Talk to individual students and see if, given two cards, they can tell you which is the higher value or if the two fractions are equivalent.

Extending the Activity: Students work individually or in small groups and place an entire pack of cards in order. Students may play a rummy-like game, collecting equivalent fractions or collecting fractions the value of which is one.

DRAW A DECIMAL

Decimal notation is very handy, but students need work in order to understand what decimals really mean. In this activity, students draw pictures of various decimal values and practice comparing those values to a whole.

From *Exploring Mathematics: Activities for Concept and Skill Development*, Copyright © 1990 Scott, Foresman and Company.

Objectives: Students will use grid paper and color in values in tenths and hundredths. They will work with concrete representations of operations with decimals.

Materials: Paper to reproduce worksheets from Teaching Aid 5.4, transparencies, overhead projector, crayons or colored pencils or markers.

Preparing for the Activity: Make transparencies of the grids that show a whole, tenths, and hundredths. Duplicate a worksheet for each student.

Conducting the Activity: Discuss with your students the idea that decimal fractions are just an extension of the place-value system with which they are already familiar. Present the fact that each place to the left has a value ten times as great as the place to the right. Review this idea by looking at place values like those below.

Place Values

hundreds	tens	ones	tenths	hundredths	thousandths
100s	10s	1s	1/10	1/100	1/1000

Project the "whole" transparency onto the chalkboard. Show where "tenths" are and what each small square represents (they're hundredths). Let students take turns shading in values such as .01, .06, .17, .29, .8, or .95.

Now ask how we could use the hundredths divisions and make thousandths and ten thousandths. [For thousandths, each hundredth could be divided into ten parts. For ten thousandths, each hundredth could be divided into 100 parts.] Students will see that both thousandths and ten thousandths are very small parts of the whole.

Present simple addition and subtraction problems with the "hundredths" transparency. For example, have a student shade .17, then shade another .35, and then find the total number of shaded squares. Try some informal multiplication and division problems—e.g., .18 divided in three pieces, six groups of .15, half of .78, and so on. Do not present rules for operations at this time. You are merely trying to get the students to picture what the problems mean.

Have the students complete the worksheet and then discuss and compare answers. They might cut out the grid with their initials and post them on a bulletin board for their classmates to see.

Here are the answers to the worksheet problems:

1. Ten squares (perhaps one row or one column) should be shaded red.
   Twenty squares (perhaps two rows or columns) should be shaded yellow.
2. Eighteen squares should be shaded blue. At this point, .52 of the total area is unshaded.
3. Twenty-five squares should be shaded brown. 1/4 = .25.
4. Five squares should be shaded orange. .05 is .1 (1/10) of—or ten times smaller than—.5.
5. One-tenth of a square should be shaded green. .001 is .01 (1/100) of .1, or .1 (1/10) of .01.

6. .41 (41 squares)
7. .11
8. .24
9. .45
10. .64 (Students might shade 80 squares and then count off eight out of each ten of these squares.)
11. Answers will vary.

Evaluating the Activity: Check the students' worksheets. Listen to their discussion and ascertain who has good ideas about decimal values.

Extending the Activity: Ask students to draw other decimal values. Provide a "hundredths" grid and let students color designs other than their initials; then have them tell what decimal fraction of the total number of squares each color covers.

+ ÷ ✕ − + − ✕ ÷ +

SPACY FRACTIONS

Most students are interested in facts about out solar system. Extend this interest with chart reading and work with fractions.

Objectives: Students will read a chart and make fractions based on information in the chart. Students will make problems based on the chart for their classmates to solve.

Materials: Paper to duplicate copies of the worksheet from Teaching Aid 5.5, planet pictures and information (optional).

Preparing for the Activity: Duplicate the worksheet. If you wish, you can augment the activity by providing pictures of the planets and reading material about our solar system.

Conducting the Activity: Encourage students to tell some of the facts they know about the planets. Pass out the worksheets and go over a few sample problems such as the ones below:

Make a fraction that compares the diameter of Mercury to the diameter of Jupiter. [Answer: 4860/140 000, which equals 243/7000]

Saturn's distance from the sun is about what fraction of Uranus's distance from the sun? [Answer: 1430/2870, or about 1/2]

Neptune's moons make up about what fraction of Uranus's moons? [Answer: 2/15]

From Exploring Mathematics: Activities for Concept and Skill Development, Copyright © 1990 Scott, Foresman and Company.

Have the students complete the worksheet. Be sure to provide some time for students to work each other's planet problems. Discuss some of their original planet problems and the answers they found.

Here are the answers to the worksheet problems:

1. Venus
2. 2400/4860; about 1/2
3. 140 000/6900; about 20 times
4. Mars and Neptune
5. 1200 km
6. 6900/227 000 000 or 69/2 270 000
7. Problems and answers will vary.

Evaluating the Activity: Check worksheet answers 1–6, and let the students check each other on 7. Observe who makes and solves challenging problems and who offers information about the planets. Observe the students' ability to find information in the chart.

Extending the Activity: Have interested students research more facts about the planets, add these facts to the chart, and make problems that involve the facts they found. Provide large paper, compasses, and string. Have students make scale models of the relative sizes of the planets using this comparison chart:

Planet	Radius of Circle (in cm)
Mercury	1
Venus	2.4
Earth	2.5
Mars	1.4
Jupiter	28
Saturn	23
Uranus	11.2
Neptune	5.1
Pluto	.5

Have students cut out the drawings, label them, and display them on the wall or in the hallway.

CHAPTER

$\boxed{5}$

TEACHING

AIDS

From *Exploring Mathematics: Activities for Concept and Skill Development*, Copyright © 1990 Scott, Foresman and Company.

FRACTION BARS

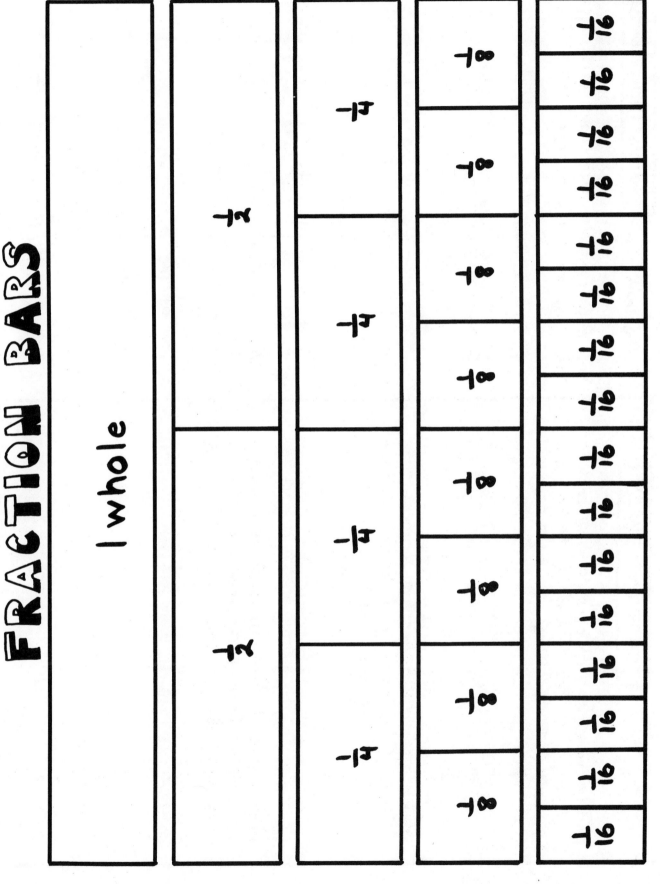

1 whole

$\frac{1}{2}$	$\frac{1}{2}$

$\frac{1}{4}$	$\frac{1}{4}$	$\frac{1}{4}$	$\frac{1}{4}$

$\frac{1}{8}$	$\frac{1}{8}$	$\frac{1}{8}$	$\frac{1}{8}$	$\frac{1}{8}$	$\frac{1}{8}$	$\frac{1}{8}$	$\frac{1}{8}$

$\frac{1}{16}$	$\frac{1}{16}$	$\frac{1}{16}$	$\frac{1}{16}$	$\frac{1}{16}$	$\frac{1}{16}$	$\frac{1}{16}$	$\frac{1}{16}$	$\frac{1}{16}$	$\frac{1}{16}$	$\frac{1}{16}$	$\frac{1}{16}$

Teaching Aid 5.1a

Problems for FRACTION BARS

Show each operation with your bars. Record the answers and a number sentence for each.

1. $\frac{1}{8}$ less than $\frac{1}{2}$

2. 6 groups of $\frac{3}{4}$

3. $\frac{1}{16}$ more than $\frac{1}{2}$

4. $\frac{1}{2}$ of a group of $\frac{3}{8}$

5. $\frac{3}{4}$ is how much larger than $\frac{1}{16}$?

6. $\frac{4}{4}$ more than $\frac{5}{8}$

7. 3 groups of $\frac{4}{4}$

8. $\frac{3}{4}$ divided into groups of 4

9. Combine $\frac{7}{8}$ and $\frac{3}{4}$

10. $\frac{3}{4}$ divided into groups of $\frac{1}{2}$

11. $\frac{1}{2}$ less than $\frac{9}{16}$

12. $\frac{5}{8}$ divided into groups of 4

Problems for FRACTION BARS

1. Use your fraction bars to show each fraction at least 2 ways. Record your results. For instance, $\frac{1}{4} = \frac{1}{8} + \frac{1}{16} + \frac{1}{16}$

$\frac{1}{8}$

$\frac{5}{16}$

$\frac{1}{2}$

2. Use the fraction bars to show each fraction. Decide if each fraction is closer to 0, $\frac{1}{2}$, or the whole.

$\frac{3}{16}$

$\frac{7}{8}$

3. Find several combinations for each fraction using the bars. Write them down. For example, $\frac{3}{8} = \frac{1}{8} + \frac{1}{8} + \frac{1}{8}$ or $\frac{3}{8} = \frac{1}{4} + \frac{1}{16} + \frac{1}{16}$

$\frac{5}{8}$

$\frac{9}{16}$

$\frac{3}{4}$

$\frac{7}{8}$

Worksheets for Fraction Bars   Teaching Aid 5.1b

From Exploring Mathematics: Activities for Concept and Skill Development, Copyright © 1990 Scott, Foresman and Company.

CLOTHESPIN FRACTION WHEEL

Write these fractions on clothespins:

$\frac{1}{8}$, $\frac{1}{4}$, $\frac{1}{2}$, $\frac{1}{3}$,

$\frac{2}{4}$, $\frac{2}{3}$, $\frac{2}{5}$,

$\frac{2}{8}$, $\frac{3}{4}$, $\frac{3}{10}$,

$\frac{4}{6}$, $\frac{4}{8}$,

$\frac{4}{10}$, $\frac{6}{8}$.

Which part is shaded? Clip on the correct clothespins.

Cut out the wheel. Color over each shaded part. Clip a clothespin or clothespins on each section.

Dial - A - Fraction

This is wheel 1. Cut it out. Use it with the other parts on the next page.

MATCH THE EQUIVALENT FRACTIONS

Teaching Aid 5.2a

FRACTION WHEELS

Dial – A – Fraction

this is wheel 2.
Cut it out.
Fasten the 3
wheels together
with a brad as
shown. Put wheel 1
on top, wheel 2
in the middle, and
wheel 3 on the
bottom.

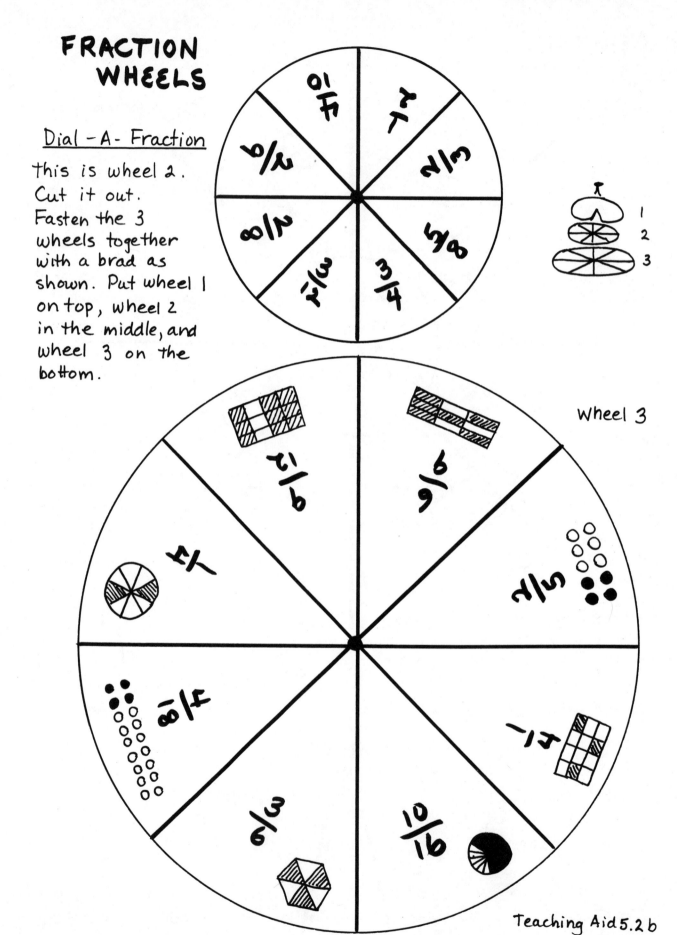

Wheel 3

Teaching Aid 5.2b

From Exploring Mathematics: Activities for Concept and Skill Development, Copyright © 1990 Scott, Foresman and Company.

$\dfrac{1}{16}$	$\dfrac{1}{8}$	$\dfrac{2}{16}$	$\dfrac{1}{6}$
$\dfrac{3}{16}$	$\dfrac{1}{4}$	$\dfrac{2}{8}$	$\dfrac{4}{16}$
$\dfrac{5}{16}$	$\dfrac{1}{3}$	$\dfrac{2}{6}$	$\dfrac{4}{12}$
$\dfrac{7}{16}$	$\dfrac{1}{2}$	$\dfrac{2}{4}$	$\dfrac{3}{6}$

Cut the cards apart.   Fraction Battle Cards   Teaching 5.3a

$\dfrac{4}{8}$	$\dfrac{6}{12}$	$\dfrac{8}{16}$	$\dfrac{2}{3}$
$\dfrac{4}{6}$	$\dfrac{5}{8}$	$\dfrac{10}{16}$	$\dfrac{3}{4}$
$\dfrac{6}{8}$	$\dfrac{12}{16}$	$\dfrac{9}{12}$	$\dfrac{7}{8}$
$\dfrac{14}{16}$	$\dfrac{15}{16}$	1	

Answer Card-
Fractions from
smallest to
largest

$\dfrac{1}{16}$, $\dfrac{1}{8}$, $\dfrac{2}{16}$, $\dfrac{3}{16}$,

$\dfrac{1}{4}$, $\dfrac{2}{8}$, $\dfrac{4}{16}$; $\dfrac{5}{16}$,

$\dfrac{1}{3}$, $\dfrac{2}{6}$, $\dfrac{4}{12}$;

$\dfrac{1}{2}$, $\dfrac{2}{4}$, $\dfrac{3}{6}$, $\dfrac{4}{8}$, $\dfrac{8}{16}$, $\dfrac{6}{12}$;

$\dfrac{2}{3}$, $\dfrac{4}{6}$; $\dfrac{3}{4}$, $\dfrac{6}{8}$, $\dfrac{9}{12}$, $\dfrac{12}{16}$;

$\dfrac{7}{8}$, $\dfrac{14}{16}$; $\dfrac{15}{16}$; 1

Teaching 5.3b

DRAW A DECIMAL

1. Color .1 red.
   Color .20 yellow.

2. Color .18 green. What decimal fraction is uncolored now? _____

3. Color $\frac{1}{4}$ of the squares brown. What is the decimal for $\frac{1}{4}$? _____

4. Color .05 orange. How does .05 compare to .5 ? _____
   _____

5. Color .001 green. How does .001 compare to .1 ? _____
   _____

   How does .001 compare to .01 ? _____
   _____

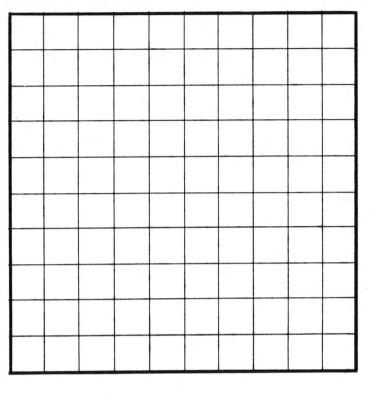

Use the grid to help you find the answers.

6. .18 + .23 _____

7. .70 − .59 _____

8. Half of .48 _____

9. 3 groups of .15 _____

10. .8 of .80 _____

11. Fill in squares to make one of your initials. What decimal fraction of the squares did you color?

   _____

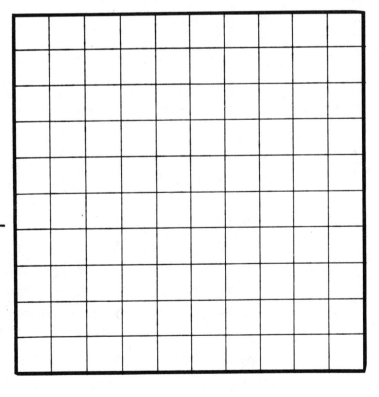

Teaching Aid 5.4

SPACY FRACTIONS

Planet	Symbol	Approximate Diameter in Kilometers	Approximate Distance from sun in 1 000 000 km	Known Number of Moons	Comments
Mercury	☿	4860	58	0	Mercury rotates only once every 59 Earth days.
Venus	♀	12000	108	0	Venus is shrouded by heavy clouds.
Earth	⊕	12800	150	1	Earth's atmosphere is mostly nitrogen and oxygen.
Mars	♂	6900	227	2	Mars has polar caps and craters on its surface.
Jupiter	♃	140 000	777	16	This largest planet has a gaseous surface.
Saturn	♄	116000	1430	20+	Saturn is known for its beautiful rings.
Uranus	♂	56000	2870	15	Uranus is also surrounded by narrow rings.
Neptune	♆	51000	4490	2	Neptune is named for the god of the sea.
Pluto	♇	2400	5900	1	Pluto's large moon is about ½ the size of the planet.

Study the chart and answer the questions
1. Which planet is about 2/3 the Earth's distance from the sun?
2. Make a fraction that compares Pluto's diameter to Mercury's. Is the fraction closer to 0, ½, or a whole?
3. Jupiter's diameter is about _____ times Mars' diameter.
4. Which planets have ⅛ the number of moons that Jupiter does?
5. What is the approximate diameter of Pluto's moon?
6. Make a fraction that compares the diameter of Mars to its approximate distance from the sun.
7. On the back of this sheet, make at least 2 problems based on the information in the chart. Ask a classmate to work your problems.

Teaching Aid 5.5

From *Exploring Mathematics: Activities for Concept and Skill Development*, Copyright © 1990 Scott, Foresman and Company.

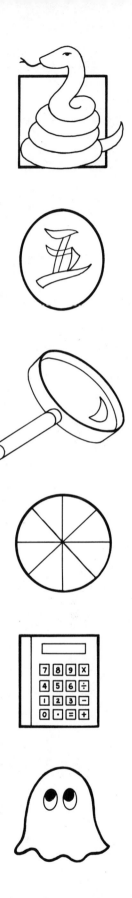

6
Dealing With Data: Graphs and Statistics

In our modern world, we're surrounded by data. From sports statistics to the number of people involved in a social or cultural activity to the numbers presented in their textbooks, children are constantly confronted by groups of numbers. Unless organized in an understandable way, big "bunches" of numbers can be hard to deal with, make sense of, and compare. Statistics and graphs help us organize numbers.

Children can start learning how to organize numerical data simply by putting numbers in order. Computation of the range of data—i.e., the difference between the highest and lowest values—gives an idea of whether numbers are "spread out" or "close together." Measures of central tendency—i.e., the mean, median, or mode of a set of data—help to give children an idea of what a typical value in the set is like.

Another common organizational device for dealing with a set of data is a graph. Graphs offer visual pictures of data relationships. Many graphs require children to categorize or group data, thereby helping to organize the data. When children make graphs of data that they collect, graph interpretation is both easy and interesting because it is based on actual experience with the numbers involved. By interpreting such graphs, children gain the experience and build the confidence needed to interpret graphs made by others.

The activities in this chapter present easy yet interesting ways to deal with data. In many of the activities, students can sharpen their decision-making skills as they select graph topics, decide how to organize data, and plan how to present data to others. Most of the activities involve group work, which not only makes the activities especially appealing to youngsters in the intermediate grades but also allows for sharing of ideas.

WEATHER DATA

The weather—it's all around us and it's always changing. Use the weather as a resource for gathering and organizing data. Although weather-observation activities are valid anytime, consider doing them especially at those times when the weather is at its most changeable and unpredictable in your area.

Objectives: Students will gather, record, and organize data on several aspects of weather—general conditions, temperature, relative humidity, wind speed, cloud types, etc.

Materials: Paper to reproduce charts (Teaching Aids 6.1b, c, d, e, f, g) and make labels for the bulletin board as suggested in Teaching Aid 6.1a, three thermometers, milk carton, rubber bands, markers.

Preparing for the Activity: Reproduce the weather charts. Prepare a bulletin board. Construct a wet-dry bulb device (or have students help you do it) to determine relative humidity. The set-up is pictured in Teaching Aid 6.1a. Divide the class into five groups.

Conducting the Activity: Review the weather-data project with the class, showing how to collect data on each of these five topics:

Indoor and Outdoor Temperatures. Students read the thermometer indoors and outdoors and fill in the graph form on Teaching Aid 6.1b.

Relative Humidity. Students observe the wet and dry bulb thermometers and use the chart on Teaching Aid 6.1a to find the approximate relative humidity. They record their data on Teaching Aid 6.1c.

Wind Speed. Students observe evidence of wind and record their findings on Teaching Aid 6.1d, using the chart on Teaching Aid 6.1e to make a judgment about wind speed.

Cloud Types. Students observe the sky and mark the date in a box on the chart (Teaching Aid 6.1f) for each type of cloud they see. Although sketches of cloud types appear along the bottom of the chart, students may also want to check pictures in a science book, encyclopedia, or other reference book.

General Weather Description. Students use words and a sketch to describe the weather and its relationship to the previous day's weather on Teaching Aid 6.1g.

Tell the children that they will work in groups and rotate through the different weather "stations" over a period of two weeks. Assign students to the different groups and then let them work for several minutes to gather their data. Ask each group to organize the data on a chart or graph and then to share their results with the class. Designate a representative from each group to show and tell about the group's results.

From *Exploring Mathematics: Activities for Concept and Skill Development,* Copyright © 1990 Scott, Foresman and Company.

You might continue this activity for a period of ten days; in that amount of time, each group could try each task twice. The first time a group completes a task is the learning experience. The second time is an opportunity for each group to refine skills and work independently. Consider using the chart below to help assign groups to tasks:

Groups

Tasks	Day 1	Day 2	Day 3	Day 4	Day 5
Temperature	A	B	C	D	E
Relative Humidity	B	C	D	E	A
Wind Speed	C	D	E	A	B
Cloud Types	D	E	A	B	C
General Description	E	A	B	C	D

Evaluating the Activity: Observe the students as they work. Do they work productively in groups? Can they read thermometers accurately? Do they complete graphs and charts correctly and neatly? Do group representatives share results in an articulate manner? How accurate are group assessments of general conditions, wind speed, and cloud types?

Extending the Activity: Add other locally available weather data to the bulletin board; the air quality index, tide information, or river stages might be pertinent. You might also use the wind chill chart from Teaching Aid 6.1e. To use the chart, students will need to determine the wind speed and outside temperature.

GUESSES

In this activity, students refine their estimating skills. In addition, they practice working with measures of central tendency and dispersion.

Objectives: Students will guess numbers of objects and outcomes of events. They will order data and determine the range, mode(s), median, and mean of a set of data.

Materials: Scrap paper, bulletin board backing and letters. For Candies in a Jar: large sealed jar full of candy. For Natural Objects: bowl filled with small natural objects (corn, pine cones, pebbles, leaves). For Bag Full of Peanuts: clear plastic bag of peanuts in the shell. For Number Cube Problems: paper to reproduce number cubes from Teaching Aid 2.1, scissors, glue.

Preparing for the Activities: Cut 5cm squares of scrap paper for students to write guesses on. Gather the materials for the different guessing experiences. Prepare a small blank bulletin board that bears the caption: "Our Guesses On . . . ."

Conducting the Activities: Display some objects or suggest problems like these:

Sports Scores. Ask students to predict the point spread for an upcoming athletic contest or the total number of points that will be scored in the game. You might use a school competition or an important professional sports event for this activity.

Candies in a Jar. Before a holiday, display a large sealed jar of candy. Let the students examine the jar, but discourage them from counting every piece. After the activity, you might have a few volunteers divide the candy equally among the students.

Natural Objects. Use a large bowl of small natural objects (kernels of corn, pine cones, pebbles, or leaves) for the guessing activity.

Bag Full of Peanuts. Show the students a large clear bag of peanuts in the shell. Have them guess not only the number of peanuts but also the total number of nuts inside the shells.

Number Cube Problems. Have students work in groups of four or five, with each group constructing two number cubes (Teaching Aid 2.1) with the numbers 1 through 6 on the faces. Talk about possible sums, toss the cubes, and then add the numbers showing on top. Ask students to predict the numbers of certain sums that they would expect in 50 tosses—e.g., perhaps they would expect ten sums of seven in the 50 tosses. After the students make their guesses, toss the cubes and tally the results. Add the numbers of sums for each group to get the actual number for the whole class.

School Attendance. Have students guess the total number of children who will be in school tomorrow.

Start each activity by having a student pass out the paper squares. Ask everyone to write his or her name along with one guess on the square. Then have the students gather around a table or open area on the floor. Have volunteers arrange the squares in order from lowest to highest.

Determine the range of guesses—the difference between the smallest and largest values. Next, arrange the paper squares in a graph-like format. If more than one student guessed the same number, put the identical guesses in a column. The resulting arrangement will clearly show a mode (or several modes). The mode is often a useful measure of central tendency. Since it is also the most frequently occurring value (or values), it shows the most "popular" choices.

Discuss the median—the middle value—and have students decide about where the median will be. To find the median, have students "count off" values from each end until they locate the middle value. If the total number of values is an even number, you can either say that the median lies between the two middle values or you can average the two middle values to determine the median.

Discuss another measure of central tendency or typical value—the mean. The mean is the arithmetic average of the set of values. Ask several students to look at the guesses and try to predict the mean. Have a pair of students use a calculator to add up the values of all the guesses and then divide by the number of guesses. If the mean results in a decimal fraction, round it to the nearest tenth or whole number. See whether anyone actually guessed the mean and—if not—who came closest to guessing it.

Finally, let a pair of students count the objects you displayed and then announce the correct number. Compare the guesses for the mode, median, and mean to the actual answer. Have each student figure out his or her deviation from the actual answer—the amount by which the guess was different from the mean.

Extend your discussion by exploring questions like the following:

What strategies did you use in making your guesses?

Does the range of guesses tend to be larger, smaller, or about the same when the numbers involved are larger? For example, would you tend to have a wider range of guesses for the total score of a soccer game or of a basketball game? Would you tend to have a wider range of guesses for a pint container of peanuts or a gallon container of small candies?

What will happen to the statistics if the "wildest" guesses—the lowest and highest—are discarded?

Evaluating the Activities: Observe the students' work and discussion to determine which students make good guesses and who can find out the range, mode, median, or mean of the data.

Extending the Activities: Let the students suggest other topics for the "Guesses" activity. Invite students to gather and display objects too. Have interested students skim the newspaper and try to find references to various measures of central tendency and range.

STEP-BY-STEP CIRCLE GRAPH

By following step-by-step instructions, students can experience success in working with circle graphs.

Objectives: Students will select topics, poll classmates, and construct and interpret circle graphs.

Materials: Paper to duplicate worksheets from Teaching Aid 6.2, material to make transparency.

Preparing for the Activity: Duplicate the worksheet and make a transparency of it as well.

Conducting the Activity: Choose 20 students to respond to a poll question, and let the rest of the class help you figuring the data and filling in the circle graph. Ask the students how large the central angles would be if a circle is divided into 20 equal sections [Answer: 18°]. Project the transparency and explain that the circle is already divided into 20 equal parts or angles of 18°.

Choose a title for the circle graph—perhaps "After School Activities"—and devise some categories for answers: homework, babysitting, other jobs, TV, telephone, sports, and "other." Poll the 20 students and tally their responses. Show the students how to write fractions for each category.

Fill in the sectors on the transparency and label each sector. Ask the class such questions as: Which activities are most popular? Are any sectors equal? Which activities are least popular? Are any sectors about one-half or one-fourth of the total?

Now let students choose topics, poll their classmates, and finish the chart and graph on the worksheet. Have the students report their findings and post their graphs on a bulletin board or in the hall.

Evaluating the Activity: Assess the students' organizational abilities: Did they pick appropriate titles and categories for their graphs? Did they complete their work accurately and in an orderly fashion? Did they share their results coherently and in an interesting manner? Spot-check the graph forms, noting correspondence of the numbers, fractions, and angles.

Extending the Activity: Let students choose a different number of people to poll. You may want to indicate that some numbers are easier to work with than others. For example, with 24 people each central angle is 15°, with 36 people each angle is 10°, and with 30 people each angle is 12°; but with 25 people each angle is 14.4° and may be harder to measure.

Have advanced students add a column to their charts and figure percentages for each sector. Starting with 20 people simplifies both computation of percentages and measurements of angles. Challenge students to show science or social studies data in circle graph form.

From *Exploring Mathematics: Activities for Concept and Skill Development*, Copyright © 1990 Scott, Foresman and Company.

POLLING PLACE

Getting the opinions of many others is a good way to gather data. But this then poses a realistic problem: How can we organize the data?

Objectives: Students will work in groups to gather, organize, and graph data. Then they will analyze their results.

Materials: Small pieces of paper, boxes, materials to decorate the boxes.

Preparing for the Activity: If necessary, secure permission to place the polling boxes and slips of paper outside your classroom.

Conducting the Activity: Organize the class into groups of four or five students. Let each group choose a topic on which to seek the opinions of other students and teachers. Some topics you might suggest include ways to improve the school, the favorite school meal, the school rule that is hardest to obey, or the favorite school subject. Students might also relate their poll topics to the results of forthcoming elections or sporting events.

Have each group decorate a poll box and decide how to pose its question. Each group must decide whether it wants to solicit free-response answers (respondents write in any answers they choose) or offer ballot-like forms that allow respondents to check just one item from a limited number of choices. Monitor each group's ideas during this phase of the activity so that the students will have usable results.

Have the groups take turns placing their polling boxes outside the classroom and inviting interested people to participate in the poll. After a day or two, each group can tabulate its results and decide how to organize the data. Each group should make some sort of graph and plan how to report the results to the class. Let group spokespersons explain the poll findings, and display the graphs outside your classroom—perhaps with a "thank you" message for those who participated.

Evaluating the Activity: Observe the groups for cooperative behavior. Who were leaders and who were followers? Note whether the groups developed good poll questions. Did groups tabulate results accurately and make reasonable graphs of their findings? Did group members convey their results clearly?

Extending the Activity: Conduct similar polls at least once more during the school year. Arrange for selected students to poll people at a shopping mall or sporting event and then to organize and report their results.

WEIGH IT, GRAPH IT

This activity lets students sharpen their measuring skills while they gain experience using many different kinds of scales. It also gives students practice in organizing and graphing data on objects they weigh.

Objectives: Students will weigh objects on various scales. They will determine intervals for the data and then graph the results.

Materials: Paper to reproduce graph forms from Teaching Aid 6.3, scales (e.g., a spring scale, balance scale and weights, fisherman's pull scale, step-on scale), five to six heavy grocery bags, classroom books.

Preparing for the Activities: Arrange to borrow various scales. Duplicate copies of the graph form.

Conducting the Activities: Announce a weighing task like those described below. Let students work a few at a time to weigh their objects. Perhaps a small group of students could use the scales while others do work in their seats. When all students have their data, have a student act as a recorder and list each mass on the chalkboard.

Determine the range of masses and the size of the intervals to use on the graph. You will be using a graph with five intervals. Usually, you divide the range of the data by five to determine the appropriate size of each interval. Some intervals are suggested for each graphing activity below.

Here are some activities you can try:

Our Writing Materials. Have each student gather all of his or her pencils, pens, and other writing materials and use a balance scale to determine the mass of these materials to the nearest gram. For intervals, you might use below 10g, 10-29g, 30-49g, 50-69g, and 70g and above.

Library Books. Let each student select two library books and weigh them on a spring scale. Intervals might be below 500g, 500-999g, 1000-1499g, 1500-1999g, and 2000g and above.

Cold Weather Clothing. On a cold day, ask each student to weigh his or her coat, hat, gloves, and other outer wear. Hang the garments from a fisherman's scale. Intervals for the clothing graph could be the same as those for the library books.

Shoes. Each student can use a spring scale to find the mass of one or both shoes. Try using the same intervals described for the library books activity.

Bag Full o' Books. Work in rows or other groups of five to seven students. Have each student in a group select a heavy book and put it in a grocery sack until the sack holds all the group's books. Next, have

From *Exploring Mathematics: Activities for Concept and Skill Development*, Copyright © 1990 Scott, Foresman and Company.

a volunteer weigh himself or herself on a step-on scale, and then weigh himself or herself a second time while holding the sack of books. Subtract the mass of the child alone from the mass of the child and book sack to determine the approximate mass of the books and bag.

Have the children make graphs of the data they found. Instruct them to fill in their intervals on the graph forms and to give each graph a title. Tell them to fill in the data that you have compiled on the chalkboard. Finally, discuss the graph results, perhaps beginning with the general question, "What does this graph tell us?"

Evaluating the Activities: Note each student's facility for using and reading the scales. Spot-check the graphs for neatness and accuracy. Observe which students seem insightful while interpreting the finished graphs.

Extending the Activities: Have students work in groups of 5-10 to determine the average (mean) mass on each exercise. Compare individual masses to the average. Which masses are quite close to the mean? Which are above or below the mean? Invite students to use calculators to find the mean for the data for the entire class. Encourage students to suggest other topics for "Weigh It" graphs.

÷×−+−×÷

CHAPTER

6

TEACHING AIDS

÷×−+−×÷

From *Exploring Mathematics: Activities for Concept and Skill Development*, Copyright © 1990 Scott, Foresman and Company.

Making A Hydrometer. To make a device to measure relative humidity, cut a slit in a plastic-coated milk carton as shown. Wrap a piece of rag around the bulb of one thermometer. Tie it with thread. Attach 2 thermometers with rubber bands. Wet the rags. Read the temperatures. Use the chart to find humidity.

wet bulb   dry bulb

temp dry bulb C°	Difference in Thermometer Readings											
	1°	2°	3°	4°	5°	6°	7°	8°	9°	10°	12°	14°
50°	94	89	84	79	74	70	65	61	57	53	46	40
45°	94	88	83	78	73	68	63	59	55	51	42	35
40°	93	88	82	77	71	65	61	56	52	47	38	31
35°	93	87	80	75	68	62	57	52	47	42	33	24
30°	92	86	78	72	65	59	53	47	41	36	26	16
25°	91	84	76	69	61	54	47	41	35	29	17	6
20°	90	81	73	64	56	47	40	32	26	18	5	
15°	89	79	68	59	49	39	30	21	12	4		
10°	87	75	62	51	38	27	17	5				

Teaching Aid 6.1a

TEMPERATURES

| Day 5 | Day 4 | Day 3 | Day 2 | Day 1 |

40°C 30° 20° 10° 0° -10° -20°

outdoor indoor

INDOOR and OUTDOOR

Date _____

Readings in degrees _____

Time of day _____

From Exploring Mathematics: Activities for Concept and Skill Development, Copyright © 1990 Scott, Foresman and Company.

Teaching Aid 6.1b

RELATIVE Humidity

Date	Dry Bulb Reading	Wet Bulb Reading	Difference	Approximate Relative Humidity
_____	_____	_____	_____	_____
_____	_____	_____	_____	_____
_____	_____	_____	_____	_____
_____	_____	_____	_____	_____
_____	_____	_____	_____	_____
_____	_____	_____	_____	_____
_____	_____	_____	_____	_____
_____	_____	_____	_____	_____
_____	_____	_____	_____	_____
_____	_____	_____	_____	_____

Teaching Aid 6.1c

WINDY WEATHER

Date	Phenomenon Observed	Approximate Wind Speed

BEAUFORT  SCALE

You can tell the wind speed by looking carefully at what's happening outdoors and using the Beaufort Wind Scale. (Pronounce it BO-fort.) The British admiral, Sir Francis Beaufort invented the scale in 1805. It works so well that scientists, weather watchers and casual observers still use it today.

BEAUFORT NUMBER	WHAT YOU'LL SEE	WIND DESCRIPTION	WIND SPEED KM/H	WIND SPEED MI/HR
0	Smoke rises straight up.	Calm	less than 2	less than 1
1	Smoke drifts slowly.	Light Air	2-5	1-3
2	Leaves rustle. Wind felt on face.	Slight Breeze	6-11	4-7
3	Leaves and twigs move. Small flags wave.	Gentle Breeze	12-19	8-12
4	Dust and paper move. Small branches move.	Moderate Breeze	20-29	13-18
5	Small trees sway. Crested waves on inland water	Fresh Breeze	30-38	19-24
6	Big branches sway. Umbrellas are hard to use.	Strong Breeze	39-50	25-31
7	Big trees sway.	High Wind	51-60	32-38
8	Twigs break off trees	Fresh Gale	61-74	39-46
9	Branches break off trees.	Strong Gale	75-86	47-54
10	Trees are uprooted. Much damage.	Whole Gale	87-100	55-63
11	Buildings damaged.	Storm	101-120	64-74
12	Extreme damage, devastation	Hurricane	Above 120	Above 74

WIND Chill Chart

Here is a wind chill Chart. Once you know the wind speed in km/h and the outdoor temperature, you can use the chart to find the wind chill temperature.

Outdoor Temperature (C°)	6	10	20	30	40	50	60	70	80	90	100
16	16	14	11	9	7	7	6	6	5	5	5
12	12	9	5	3	1	0	0	-1	-1	-1	-1
8	8	5	0	-3	-5	-6	-7	-7	-8	-8	-8
4	4	0	-5	-8	-11	-12	-13	-14	-14	-14	-14
0	0	-4	-10	-14	-17	-18	-19	-20	-21	-21	-21
-4	-4	-8	-15	-20	-23	-25	-26	-27	-27	-27	-27
-8	-8	-13	-21	-25	-29	-31	-32	-33	-34	-34	-34
-12	-12	-17	-26	-31	-35	-37	-39	-40	-40	-40	-40
-16	-16	-22	-31	-37	-41	-43	-45	-46	-47	-47	-47
-20	-20	-26	-36	-43	-47	-49	-51	-52	-53	-53	-53
-24	-24	-31	-42	-48	-53	-56	-58	-59	-60	-60	-60

Wind Speed in Kilometers / Hour

Teaching Aid 6.1e

CL8UD TYPES

No Clouds	Overcast	Stratus	Cumulus	Nimbus	Cirrus

From Exploring Mathematics: Activities for Concept and Skill Development, Copyright © 1990 Scott, Foresman and Company.

WHAT'S THE  WEATHER LIKE?

Date	General Description	Sketch	Comparison of Today's Weather to Yesterday's

Teaching Aid 6.1g

STEP BY STEP CIRCLE GRAPH

Category	Number	Fraction	Angle
Totals	20	$\frac{20}{20}$	360°

title _____

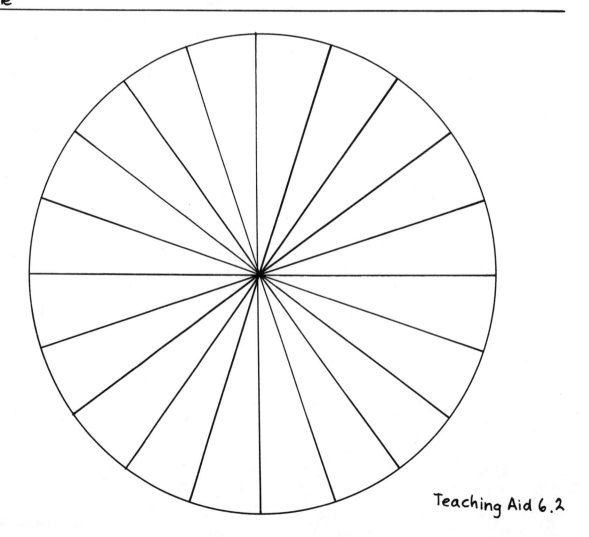

Teaching Aid 6.2

From *Exploring Mathematics: Activities for Concept and Skill Development*, Copyright © 1990 Scott, Foresman and Company.

Graph Title

Categories

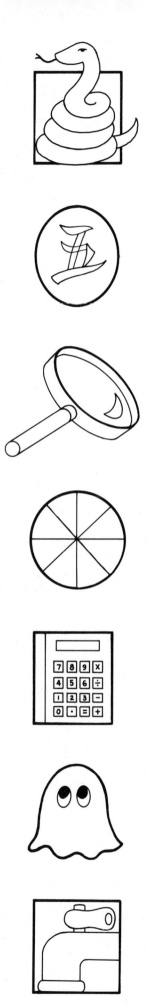

7
Exploring Shapes: Geometry

Geometry constitutes an important part of mathematics education in the intermediate grades. Study of geometry helps children understand the shapes they encounter in the world around them. In addition, development of a meaningful vocabulary of geometric terms helps students communicate precisely about shapes, positions, and relationships.

Geometric thinking is different from numerical thinking. Some students who struggle with numbers excel at geometry. This is yet another way in which the study of geometry balances and enriches the mathematics curriculum.

In their study of geometry, students in the intermediate grades extend and refine their study of plane figures, moving naturally into work with space or three-dimensional figures. Students also can explore concepts of area and perimeter in concrete ways. Work with drawing and constructing helps students learn about and retain geometric concepts. Discussion of problem situations and of problems with several correct answers also enhances learning. The activities in this chapter will extend and deepen your students' exploration of geometry.

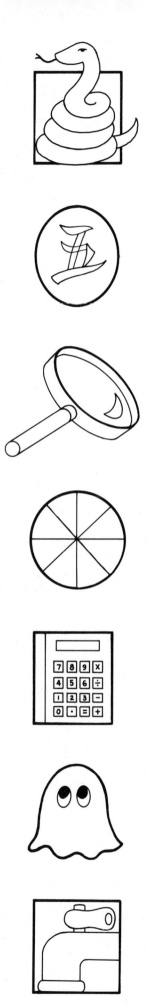

GEOMETRY BOOKLETS

Making drawings is one valuable way for students to show what they are learning. Geometry booklets let students compile and organize their drawings.

Objectives: Students will draw and label pictures of the geometric figures they are studying.

Materials: Plain paper for each student to make a booklet, rulers, pencils.

Preparing for the Activity: Decide which geometric figures students will be studying and should include in their geometry booklets.

Conducting the Activity: Tell the students that they will compile an illustrated booklet of the geometric figures they will be studying in their geometry unit. Show them how to fold paper in half crosswise to make a four-page booklet. Each page can contain one or more labeled drawings. For example, booklets might contain carefully drawn pictures of different kinds of polygons (triangles, quadrilaterals, pentagons, hexagons, and so on), angles (acute, obtuse, right, straight), or specific kinds of polygons (equilateral, right, scalene, and isosceles triangles, or quadrilaterals such as parallelograms, rhombi, squares, and rectangles). The students should label each figure with its name and perhaps with a statement of essential characteristics.

   Tell the students that they may also include in their booklets creative designs featuring some of the geometric figures they are studying. Collect and check the booklets. Encourage students to show each other some of the figures they have drawn. Display unusual designs on a reading table or bulletin board.

Evaluating the Activity: Check the booklets for neatness, accuracy, and completeness. Include some labeled drawings on your unit test.

Extending the Activity: Ask students to suggest other items for their geometry booklets. Make student suggestions a required or optional part of the assignment.

COORDINATE PICTURES

Pictures emerge quickly as students plot points and join the points with line segments.

Objectives: Students will follow directions in order to plot the correct points to make pictures.

Materials: Paper to duplicate coordinate picture worksheets from Teaching Aid 7.1b and c, transparency to reproduce the graph grid from Teaching Aid 7.1a, overhead projector, marker for overhead projector.

Preparing for the Activity: Duplicate copies of student instructions for coordinate pictures from Teaching Aid 7.1b and c. Make a transparency of the graph grid (Teaching Aid 7.1a).

Conducting the Activity: If your students are unfamiliar with locating points in a plane by coordinates, introduce the idea to them. Project the graph grid onto the chalkboard. Draw in axes (you will work only with the first quadrant), and number along each axis from 0 to 10. Show and name several points and see if the students can tell how you are naming them—e.g., the point (3,7) is 3 spaces to the right and 7 spaces up; the point (8,5) is 8 spaces to the right and 5 spaces up. Let the students locate and name several points, including ones like (0,5), (0,0), or (3,0). Talk about typical places where two coordinates are used to locate points—on road maps or seats in an auditorium for instance.

Now introduce the idea of making a coordinate picture. Students will plot points in order and connect the points as they go along. Help the students complete the sample picture (a cat's face) by working together. Then students can work on their own to finish one or more coordinate pictures. Circulate around the classroom as the students work. Since you will be able to see at a glance areas where students make errors, you will find it easy to guide them. Have students color their completed pictures and display them on a bulletin board.

Here are the answers to Teaching Aids 7.1b and c:

7.1b

7.1c

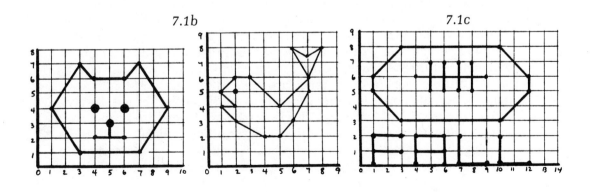

Evaluating the Activity: Look over the pictures to see what points are plotted and joined correctly. Notice which students work quickly, accurately, and independently.

Extending the Activity: Make other pictures or simple messages for the students. Encourage able and interested students to create coordinate pictures for their classmates to use.

+ ÷ ✕ − + − ✕ ÷ +

EASY POLYHEDRONS

If students work carefully, they'll see two-dimensional patterns "shape up" to become three-dimensional geometric figures!

Objectives: Students will construct polyhedrons and a cylinder model from patterns. They will determine the number of faces, edges, and angles each figure has.

Materials: Paper to duplicate copies of polyhedron patterns (Teaching Aids 7.2a, b, and c), and the faces/angles/edges chart (Teaching Aid 7.2d), scissors, glue, needles and thread (optional).

Preparing for the Activity: Duplicate copies of the polyhedron patterns. Make up a model or two. Duplicate a faces/angles/edges chart for each group of four or five students.

Conducting the Activity: Show the students a completed model. Instruct them to cut out the patterns carefully and crease them along the lines. Students should glue only a few tabs at a time, hold those "joints" carefully to let them set, and then glue and set a few more tabs. Emphasize that making neat models requires careful work.

Have the students complete several models (they may need several sessions to complete all the models), and display the finished models on a table or shelf. Let the students match the name tags to the models. If you wish to hang the models from a bulletin board or suspend them from the ceiling, show the students how to thread a needle with about one meter of thread. Then instruct them to stitch through a corner of a model, pulling most of the thread through and leaving about 6cm hanging. At this point, tell them to cut off and knot the thread, leaving a thread hanger about 5cm long. The long piece of thread that remains in the needle may be used to make hangers for other models.

Using the students' models (and other objects from the classroom), have the students work in groups to examine the polyhedrons. Tell them

From *Exploring Mathematics: Activities for Concept and Skill Development*, Copyright © 1990 Scott, Foresman and Company.

to determine the numbers of faces (flat or plane surfaces), edges (line segments where two faces meet), and angles (three-dimensional angles where faces meet) each model or classroom object has. The groups should carefully count the faces, edges, and angles and record the data on the chart. If the students have problems remembering which parts they have counted, have them mark each part lightly with a felt-tip marker as they do their counting.

Ask the students to examine their data and see if they find any patterns. One way of interpreting the data pattern is to note that the number of angles plus the number of faces for any figure equals the number of edges plus two $(a + f) = (e + 2)$. The chart below shows the number of faces, angles, and edges for each model.

	Faces	Number of Edges	Angles
Tetrahedron	4	6	4
Pyramid with square base	5	8	5
Cube	6	12	8
Cylinder	2	0	0
Prism with rectangular base	6	12	8
Prism with hexagonal base	8	18	12

Evaluating the Activity: Check the students' models for sharp creases, straight edges, and careful gluing. Observe the students as they identify models, and see that they do so accurately.

Extending the Activity: Allow students to decorate their models with designs or glued-on glitter. Display the models on a holiday tree. Challenge interested students to make their own patterns for models; this will require creative planning and careful measuring. Draw the attention of all students to examples of cylinders and polyhedrons in the environment.

PERIMETERS EVERYWHERE

This activity emphasizes understanding the concept of perimeter, and it provides lots of measurement practice.

Objectives: Students will measure and compute perimeters of various objects.

Materials: Paper to reproduce recording forms from Teaching Aid 7.3, meter sticks, trundle wheel (optional), 20 or 30cm rulers, yarn, scissors.

Preparing for the Activities: Duplicate a copy of the recording form for each group of three to four students. Gather several meter sticks. If possible, obtain a trundle wheel. Have students supply their own 20 or 30cm rulers as well as 20 to 30 objects to display on a table.

Conducting the Activities: Review the concept of perimeter—the linear distance around an object or the sum of the lengths of line segments in a polygon. Organize students in groups of three or four, and have them complete activities such as the following.

Perimeters of Classroom Objects. Using the objects displayed on the table, students select at least ten, estimate and measure perimeters, and record their data.

Perimeters in the School. Groups of students determine the different perimeters of various locations in the school: classroom, library, hallways, gymnasium, cafeteria, or even an outdoor playing field. They can use meter sticks or trundle wheels to measure off the distances. Allow the groups to report their findings to the class.

Smaller Classroom Perimeters. Groups of students choose one or two locations in the classroom (window panes, desk tops, bulletin boards, floor tiles, bookcases, etc.) and measure the perimeters. Then they outline the perimeters with yarn and post little signs on the perimeters for their classmates to read and think about.

Perimeter Search. Each student cuts a 30cm length of yarn and then searches at home for an object that has a 30cm perimeter as well as for objects with greater and lesser perimeters. Students can display their objects—or descriptions or pictures of their objects—on a table or bulletin board. Use three categories: "Objects Having a 30cm Perimeter," "Objects with Perimeters Less Than 30cm," and "Objects with Perimeters Greater Than 30cm."

Evaluating the Activities: Circulate through the classroom as the students are working in order to spot-check their skill in using measuring tools and their understanding of perimeter. Spot-check the students' recording forms and the perimeters of the objects they bring from home.

Extending the Activities: Vary each activity to focus on area rather than perimeter. Use an area of 100cm² for an "Area Search" at home.

From *Exploring Mathematics: Activities for Concept and Skill Development,* Copyright © 1990 Scott, Foresman and Company.

COMPARING PERIMETERS AND AREAS

By coloring the perimeters and areas of figures, students can see the difference between the two measurements quite vividly. In this activity, students work with both perimeter and area, comparing the two as they work.

Objectives: Students will cut polygons from squared paper, color the perimeters and areas of their figures, and then estimate and determine the perimeters and areas.

Materials: Paper to reproduce worksheets (from Teaching Aids 7.4a and b) and grid paper (from Teaching Aid 7.1a), scissors, glue, red and blue crayons or markers or colored pencils.

Preparing for the Activities: Duplicate the worksheets and centimeter square paper.

Conducting the Activities: Review the ideas of perimeter and area. Perimeter is the distance around a polygon or the sum of the lengths of the line segments that make up a polygon. Area is the surface "covered" by the polygon or the number of square units in the interior of the polygon.

  Have the students use the centimeter squared paper and outline a 2cm x 3cm rectangle in red. Then tell them to find the perimeter of the rectangle. Some will count the number of line segments. Others may add 2 + 3 + 2 + 3. Still others may work with (2 x 2) + (2 x 3). The perimeter is 10cm.

  Now have the students shade the interior of the rectangle blue and determine its area (6cm²). Then have the students draw an "odd-shaped" figure, color its perimeter and area, and determine the perimeter and area. The polygon below is a decagon (10-sided figure) with a perimeter of 14cm and an area of 8cm².

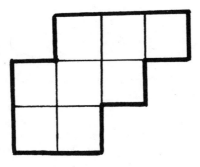

Have the students complete either or both worksheets (Teaching Aid 7.4a and b), using the rest of their sheet of squared paper to cut the required polygons. Have the students check their own answers and discuss some of their different answers and ways of thinking about the problems. Although you probably will not want to present formulas in a formal way at this point, encourage any students who seem ready to talk about the shortcuts or formulas they used for finding perimeter and area of rectangles.

Here are the answers to Teaching Aid 7.4a:

1. Figure A: P = 30cm; A = 22cm²
   Figure B: P = 28cm; A = 24cm²
2. Estimates will vary.
   Areas will vary.
3. Perimeters will vary.
4. Perimeters and areas will vary.

Here are the answers to Teaching Aid 7.4b:

1. Answers will vary.
2. Rectangles (and other polygons) will vary, but each area should be 24cm². Some typical rectangles might be 3x8cm, 2x12cm, 4x6cm. Perimeters will vary.
3. The shapes of the polygons will vary, but the perimeters should be 16cm. Some typical rectangles might be 4x4cm, 7x1cm, 6x2cm, 5x3cm. Areas will vary.

Evaluating the Activities: Observe students as they work and see who seems to have perimeter and area concepts firmly in mind. Spot-check the students' computation of perimeters and area. Include some concrete problems on perimeter and area on your next test. Pay attention to the students' neatness in completing their polygons.

Extending the Activities: Work with similar problems, and encourage the students to use some diagonal lines. They will have to measure the diagonals in determining perimeters and make estimates of areas. Invite students to make *many* rectangles of a given perimeter or area and see what patterns they can find when they compare the perimeters or areas.

Have students name the polygons they draw, using the names quadrilateral, pentagon, hexagon, heptagon, octagon, nonagon, and decagon. For polygons with more than ten sides, use names like "11-gon" and "20-gon."

From *Exploring Mathematics: Activities for Concept and Skill Development*, Copyright © 1990 Scott, Foresman and Company.

÷ ✕ − + − ✕ ÷

CHAPTER

7

TEACHING

AIDS

÷ ✕ − + − ✕ ÷

CENTIMETER GRID

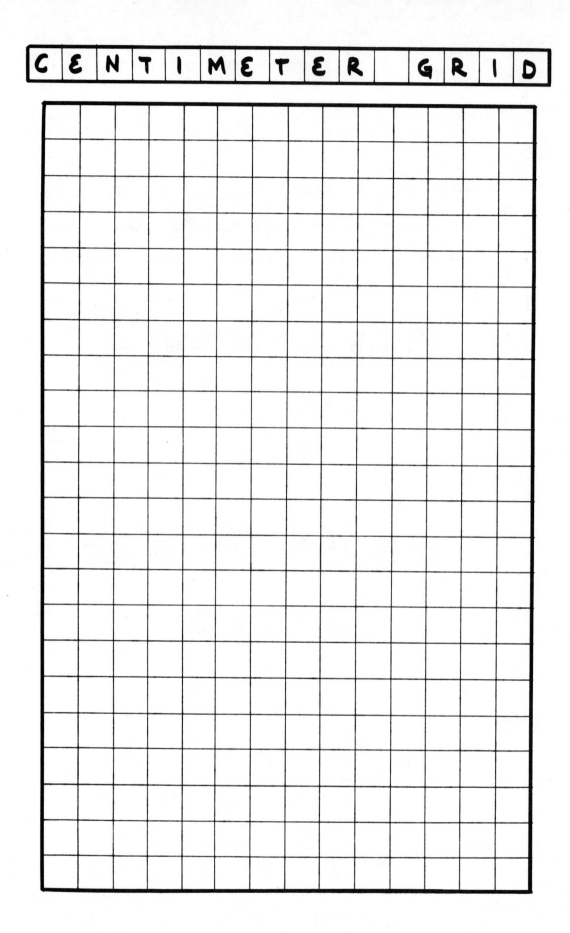

Teaching Aid 7.1a

C O O R D I N A T E Pictures

Here's how to draw a
coordinate picture.
1. Number 0-10 on the
   horizontal axis and 0-8
   on the vertical axis.
2. Plot these points. As
   you go along, connect
   them with line segments.

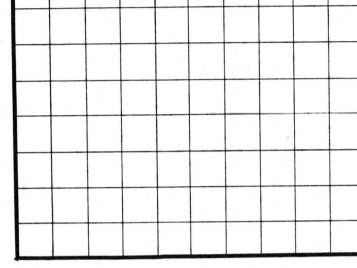

   1. (1,4)   6. (9,4)
   2. (3,7)   7. (7,1)
   3. (4,6)   8. (3,1)
   4. (6,6)   9. (1,4)
   5. (7,7)

3. Place large dots at (4,4)
   and (6,4). Draw a line segment from (5,3) to (5,2). Draw
   another segment from (4,2) to (6,2).
4. You should see the face of a familiar animal.

Here's how to make another
picture. It's an aquatic
creature.
1. Number 0-9 on each axis.
2. Plot these points. Connect
   them with line segments as
   you go along.

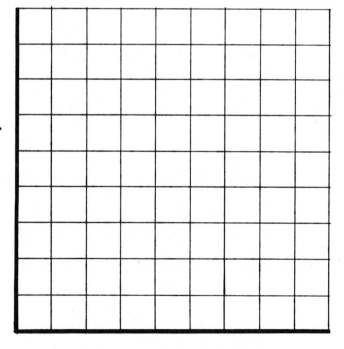

   1. (1,5)   10. (7,5)
   2. (2,6)   11. (6,3)
   3. (3,6)   12. (5,2)
   4. (5,4)   13. (4,2)
   5. (7,6)   14. (2,3)
   6. (6,8)   15. (1,4)
   7. (7, 7½) 16. (2,4)
   8. (8,8)   17. (1,5)
   9. (7,6)

3. Make a large dot at (2,5)

Teaching Aid 7.1b

C O O R D I N A T E Picture

Here's a picture of a familiar object used in a sport.
Below it is the name of the season in which the sport is
played the most. To create the picture, follow the directions.

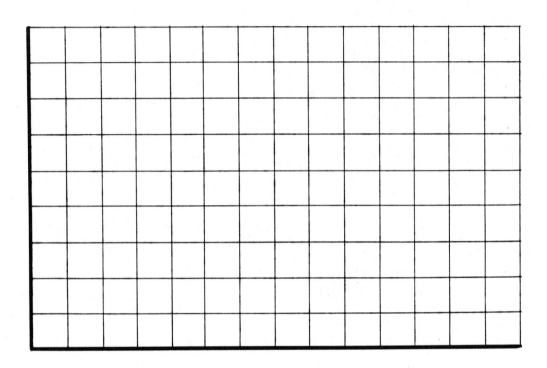

1. Number 0-14 on the horizontal axis and 0-9 on the
   vertical axis.

2. Join these points in order:

   (1,5)   (1,6)   (3,8)   (10,8)   (12,6)   (12,5)   (10, 3)   (3,3)

3. Now join each pair of points.

   (4,6) to (9,6)   (5,7) to (5,5)   (6,7) to (6,5)

   (7,7) to (7,5)   (8,7) to (8,5)

4. Now spell a word by drawing in these line segments:

   (1,2) to (1,0)   (1,1) to (3,1)   (1,2) to (3,2)

   (4,2) to (6,2)   (4,2) to (4,0)   (6,2) to (6,0)

   (4,1) to (6,1)   (7,2) to (7,0)   (7,0) to (9,0)

   (10,2) to (10,0)   (10,0) to (12,0)   Teaching Aid 7.1c

From *Exploring Mathematics: Activities for Concept and Skill Development*, Copyright © 1990 Scott, Foresman and Company.

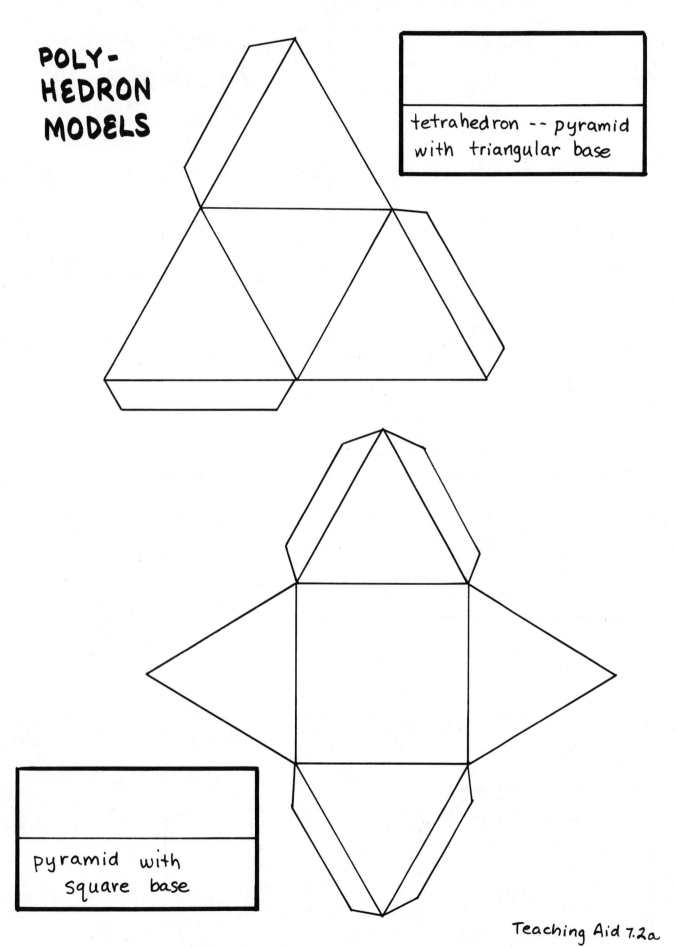

POLY-
HEDRON
MODELS

tetrahedron -- pyramid
with triangular base

pyramid with
square base

Teaching Aid 7.2a

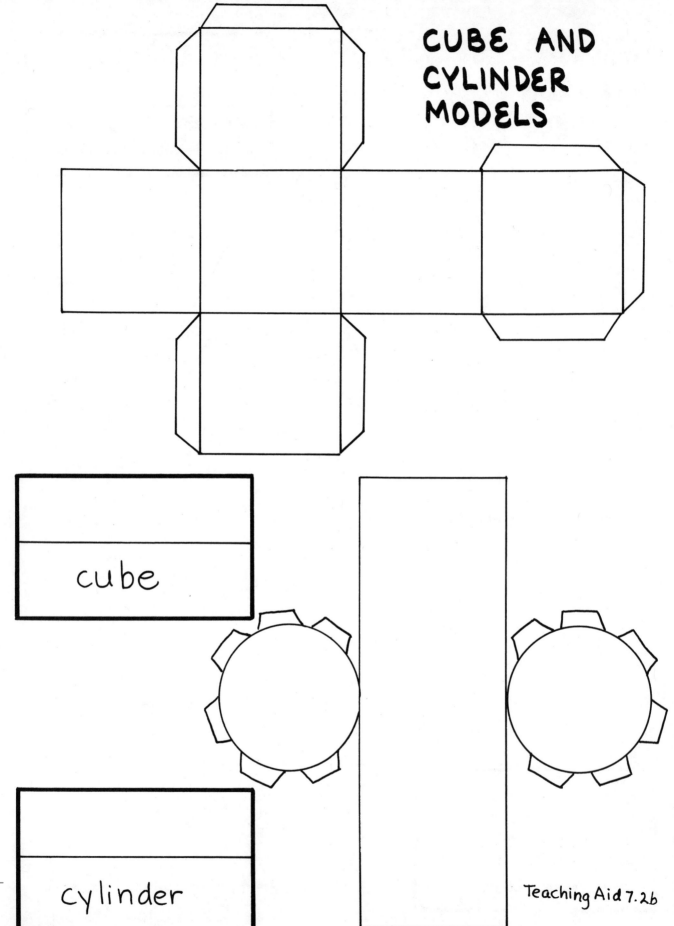

CUBE AND
CYLINDER
MODELS

cube

cylinder

Teaching Aid 7.2b

POLYHEDRON MODELS

prism with
rectangle base

prism with
hexagon base

Teaching Aid 7.2c

POLYHEDRON Count - Down

Geometric Solid	Number of Faces	Number of Edges	Number of Angles
Tetrahedron			
Pyramid with Square Base			
Cube			
Cylinder			
Prism with Rectangular Base			
Prism with Hexagon Base			
Another from your room _____			
Another from your room _____			

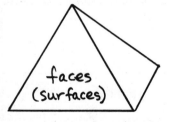

faces (surfaces)

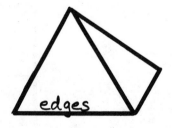

edges

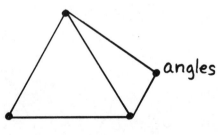

angles

Teaching Aid 7.2d

From Exploring Mathematics: Activities for Concept and Skill Development, Copyright © 1990 Scott, Foresman and Company.

PERIMETERS   Small Objects

group names _____

name of Object	estimated perimeter	actual perimeter
1. _____	_____	_____
2. _____	_____	_____
3. _____	_____	_____
4. _____	_____	_____
5. _____	_____	_____
6. _____	_____	_____
7. _____	_____	_____
8. _____	_____	_____
9. _____	_____	_____
10. _____	_____	_____

Teaching Aid 7.3

COMPARING PERIMETER AND AREA

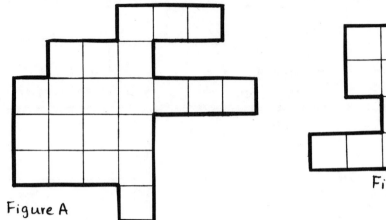

Figure A

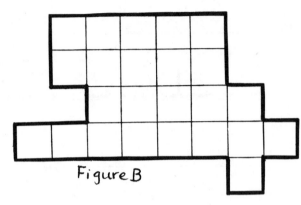

Figure B

1. Color the perimeter of each figure red. Color the area blue.
   Count segments to find the perimeter of each.
   Count squares to find the area of each. Fill in the chart.

	Figure A	Figure B
perimeter		
area		

2. Use centimeter square paper. Cut out a figure with perimeter = 20cm. Glue it below. Shade the area blue.
   Estimate the area: _____ cm²
   Actual area: _____ cm²

3. Use centimeter square paper. Cut out a figure with area = 8cm². Glue it below. Color the perimeter red.
   Estimate the perimeter: _____ cm
   Actual perimeter: _____ cm

4. Cut out any figure that will fit in the space below. Glue it in place. Fill in the chart.

	Estimated	Actual
perimeter		
area		

Teaching Aid 7.4a

COMPARING PERIMETER AND AREA

1. Cut 2 polygons from centimeter squared paper. Draw around each shape's perimeter -- its outline -- in red. Shade in its area -- its interior -- with blue. Glue your polygons below.

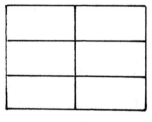

2. Cut out at least 2 different polygons with areas = 24cm². Glue them below. Figure and record their areas and perimeters.

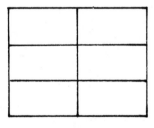

3. Cut out at least 2 different polygons with perimeters = 16cm. Glue them below. Figure and record their perimeters and areas.

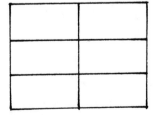

Teaching Aid 7.4b

8

Learning by Doing: Building Measurement Skills

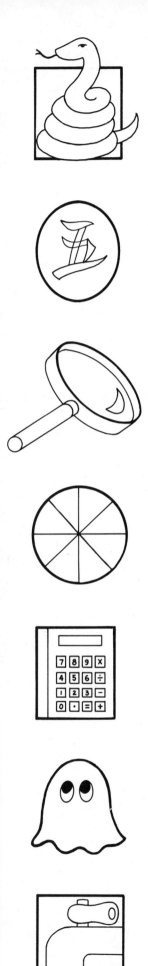

Children in the intermediate grades are working toward more independent use of measuring tools and using measuring tools with more precision than they did in the early grades. Fourth, fifth, and sixth grade students typically refine their use of measuring tools. For example, they can "read" rulers and draw line segments to the nearest millimeter. Their work with measurements of length extends beyond centimeters and millimeters to the use of decimeters, meters, dekameters, and kilometers. Students also deal with measures of temperature, volume, and mass.

Students learn to measure by becoming involved in measuring. As they work with measuring tools, students should record data and discuss their results. Writing and talking about measuring help students with their awareness of what they are doing. Hands-on experiences with measurement also help students build mental images of units of measurement.

Students should estimate whenever possible before they measure. The few moments students spend on estimating pay great dividends in generating interest in the actual answers and in encouraging students to "read" measuring tools accurately. When students make some of their own measuring tools, they gain insight into the process of calibrating a tool. In addition to taking pride in making useful tools, the students produce usable equipment which they can also use at home.

This chapter offers some involving activities that encourage students to explore measurement in meaningful ways. As they complete the activities, students record data and use basic math skills, construct and use measuring devices in a variety of ways, and learn by doing through participating in a wide range of interesting exercises.

MAKE YOUR OWN MEASURING TAPE

When children make their own measuring tapes, they not only produce usable equipment but also learn a lot in the process.

Objectives: Students will construct 10cm and 1m measuring tapes; they will use the tapes for experiences in estimating and measuring lengths.

Materials: Paper to reproduce patterns and task cards from Teaching Aid 8.1a and b, crayons, scissors, pens, clear tape or contact paper.

Preparing for the Activity: Reproduce patterns and task cards.

Conducting the Activity: Have the students color the tape sections and then carefully cut them out and number each section. Next, have them tape the sections together, placing the end marks of the sections on top of each other. Help the children reinforce their tape measures with a backing of clear tape, masking tape, or contact paper.

Let the students tell what they have learned. They should know that 10cm = 1dm and 10dm = 1m, and they should have a clear mental image of the lengths of 1cm, 1dm, and 1m. Have small groups use the tapes to measure classroom objects as suggested on the task cards.

Evaluating the Activity: Did the children produce neat, clearly labeled, usable tapes? Were they able to express relationships of measures? Did they make reasonable estimates of lengths? Did they use their tapes accurately to measure objects?

Extending the Activity: Interested students can make more task cards for their classmates to use. Have students take their measuring tapes home and measure family members, furniture, and other objects.

From *Exploring Mathematics: Activities for Concept and Skill Development*, Copyright © 1990 Scott, Foresman and Company.

TEMPERATURE COLLAGE

This activity helps to enhance children's mental images of different temperatures and the temperatures associated with various conditions.

Objectives: Students will construct and set a thermometer model; they will draw and find pictures of conditions associated with different temperatures.

Materials: Paper to reproduce thermometer models from Teaching Aid 8.2, old newspapers and catalogs and magazines, scissors.

Preparing for the Activity: Duplicate the thermometer model worksheet so that each student has a copy.

Conducting the Activity: Instruct the students to cut the "mercury" from the side of their worksheets and insert it in the slit of the thermometers. Let them set the thermometer to various levels and tell each other the temperature readings. Discuss various temperature readings, and have the students set their thermometers as you go along.

Here are some examples of temperature readings you can use:

Water freezes at this temperature. Set your thermometer. [0° C]

You'd want to wear a light jacket if the thermometer read this temperature. [about 10° to 15° C]

The thermometer might read this temperature inside a freezer. [about -5° to -20° C]

Set your thermometer to the highest temperature we will likely have outdoors this summer. [Answers will vary from about 28° to 40° C depending on your area.]

Make a guess about today's temperature outdoors and set your thermometer. [Check an outdoors thermometer and announce the temperature. Have the students reset their thermometers to the correct current temperature.]

Water boils at about this temperature. [100° C]

An iced drink would have about this temperature. [about 3° to 8° C]

Set your thermometer to normal body temperature. [37° C]

Have the students suggest other temperatures and conditions for which they can set their thermometer models. Then have them glue or draw six to eight small pictures on their thermometer models and draw arrows to the different temperatures associated with the conditions in their pictures. Interested students can even consult an encyclopedia to research temperatures in different geographic areas and use pictures of these areas on their thermometer models.

Evaluating the Activity: On your next test, include items about different temperatures and reading thermometers. Observe the children's work: Did they set their models correctly? Did they pick or draw appropriate pictures for different temperatures?

Extending the Activity: Make a larger thermometer model as part of a bulletin board. Have students post pictures for various conditions associated with temperatures near the thermometer. Make a more thorough study of typical temperatures around the world or in countries you are studying. Attach thermometer models set to typical temperatures to a map showing other countries.

TEMPERATURE SCAVENGER HUNT

Students should find a wide range of temperatures as they "scavenge" in various locations throughout the school.

Objectives: Students will work in groups to read thermometers and record data.

Materials: Paper to reproduce worksheets from Teaching Aid 8.3, thermometers, hot plate and pan of water, container of ice.

Preparing for the Activity: Add two locations in the blank spaces of the recording form. If your students have access to a freezer or cold storage room, be sure to add such a site to the hunt. Duplicate a recording form for each group of four or five students. Set up a hot plate and container of ice.

Conducting the Activity: Work with students to read the thermometer in several settings. Consider using the large thermometer model from the "Temperature Collage" activity.

Establish rules of conduct for the scavenger hunt: groups must stay together, complete their out-of-the-classroom work and return to the classroom as quickly as possible, whisper as they work, share the work load, and so on. If you have a thermometer for each group, all the students may work on the scavenger hunt at the same time; if not, have groups take turns.

Check with the children as they work. If you find unreasonable answers (such as 25° for ice water), check both the thermometer itself (it

From Exploring Mathematics: Activities for Concept and Skill Development, Copyright © 1990 Scott, Foresman and Company.

might be broken) and the children's understanding of how to read the thermometer. When all groups have finished the scavenger hunt, discuss some of the results. Focus on a location or two and examine the range of temperatures found there. Let students share their findings, telling the locations they used and the temperatures they found. Discuss reasons for small variations in the readings for the same locations.

Evaluating the Activity: Spot-check the recording forms. Check with groups as they work, and make sure that each child can read the thermometer.

Extending the Activity: Ask groups for suggestions of other places to take temperatures. Estimate and measure room temperature from time to time. Read about temperatures in other cities in the newspaper. Ask students to listen to or watch national weather reports and notice the wide range in temperatures across the country.

CALIBRATE A CUP

Objectives: Students will calibrate cups in 30ml intervals and then read the cups' scales in various activities.

Materials: Transparent plastic cups, masking tape, 15ml spoons or small calibrated cups (many medicine cups are calibrated in milliliters), scissors, ballpoint pens or fine-line permanent markers, four or five large jars or pitchers of water, paper towels.

Preparing for the Activity: Set out supplies for the students.

Conducting the Activity: Divide the class into groups of six or eight students. Have each group take turns calibrating cups according to the following procedure:

1. Put a strip of masking tape vertically on the side of the cup.
2. Pour water into the cup 30ml at a time.
3. Mark the water level on the tape after each addition of water.
4. Number the marks.
5. Write "ml" at the top of the tape to indicate the unit of measurement.
6. Pour "left over" water back into the pitcher.

Now have the groups take turns filling their cups to various levels and telling each other how many milliliters of water their cups contain. Give some instructions such as:

"Fill your cups to 45ml."

"Fill your cups to about 20ml."

"Fill your cups to 60ml, and then try to pour out about 30ml of water. Check to see what your cups now read."

Around lunch time, have the students clean their cups. Pour milk or juice into their cups, perhaps filling the cups to the 120ml mark. Then have each student take one swallow, note the new level of the liquid, and figure about how many milliliters of the liquid he or she drank. Students should continue the activity until their cups are empty. They can then figure the average number of milliliters per swallow. Write some of the average numbers on the chalkboard and examine the range and median of the data. Finally, allow the students to take their cups home with them.

Evaluating the Activity: Observe the students' work: Did they work neatly and cooperatively? Were their measures reasonably accurate? Did they work confidently and accurately in reading measures and filling their cups to various levels?

Extending the Activity: Ask the students for suggestions regarding ways to use their cups for classroom or home activities. Use the cups with "solid fluids" such as rice, cornmeal, or birdseed. Have the children take handfuls of the fluids, estimate their volume, and then pour the fluids into the cups and take a measurement. Assign the students to use their cups at home and school for keeping track of their total daily liquid intake. After three or four days of recording their liquid intake, the students can discuss and compare their data.

SHRINK-A-SHAPE

Objectives: Students will draw, cut, and measure small shapes. Then they will shrink the shapes and measure them again.

Materials: Paper to duplicate instructions (Teaching Aid 8.4a) and worksheets (Teaching Aid 8.4b), toaster oven, aluminum foil, three or four clean Styrofoam food trays per student (possibly supplied by students), rulers calibrated in millimeters, markers, scissors.

Preparing for the Activity: Duplicate a copy of the instructions and a worksheet for each student.

Conducting the Activity: Ask students to carefully draw a 10cm (100mm x 100mm) square on Styrofoam. Students may find it easier to draw on the Styrofoam if they first trim the edges off their food trays. After drawing their squares, students should cut them out, measure their depth in millimeters, and record information about them on their worksheets.

Now the fun begins! Working in a well-ventilated area, have the students decorate their squares any way they wish. Then place several squares on a piece of foil and bake them at 350° F (175° C) for 20 to 30 seconds. Let the students watch through the oven's glass door so that they can see their shapes shrink. Take the shapes out of the oven, let them cool for several seconds, and then lift them off the foil.

After the students have had an opportunity to admire their shapes, they should sketch the results on the worksheet and record their measurements. Help the students complete the fractional statements about the dimensions of their shapes; if they are familiar with decimals, have them use decimals in the statements.

Encourage the students to repeat the process using a different shape. Large, simple shapes work best. If students want to make shrink-a-shape "charms" to hang on a necklace or bracelet, have them cut a hole 1cm x 1cm near the top of their shape. The hole, along with the rest of the charm, will shrink to a size suitable for threading onto yarn or string.

Occasionally, shrink-a-shape pieces will wrinkle or even collapse. If this happens, allow students to make replacements.

Evaluating the Activity: Observe students to see that they work cooperatively and safely. Spot-check the worksheets to see that measurements and fractions are reasonable.

Extending the Activity: Let students make a variety of decorative shapes and use their creations in an art project.

÷ ✕ − ✛ − ✕ ÷

CHAPTER

TEACHING AIDS

MAKE YOUR OWN MEASURING TAPE

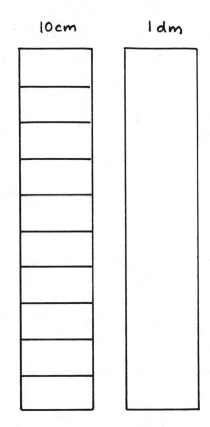

10cm   1dm

For the 10cm and 1dm tapes, color the sections, then cut out the pieces. Number and label each section with a unit.

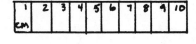

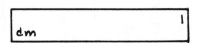

For the 1m tape, color one part and leave the other plain. Cut apart all 10 pieces and tape them together overlapping in the overlap area. Number each section and label the tape with its unit. Reinforce the tape with clear tape or contact paper.

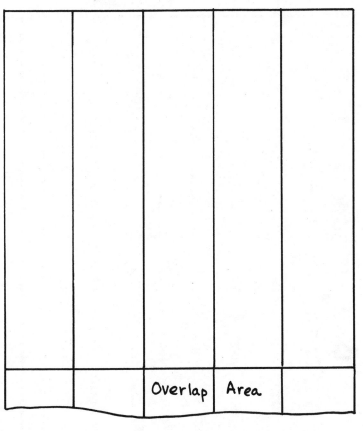

Ten pieces to make the 1m tape

Teaching Aid 8.1a

Body Measures

Use your 1m tape to measure:

	estimate	actual
Around your head		
Around your waist		
Around your wrist		
Around your ankle		

Write your measures in order, smallest first

from your Desk or Notebook I

Use your 10cm or 1m tape.
Measure each object.

	estimate	actual
Length of sheet of paper		
Width of sheet of paper		
Length of dictionary or reference book		
Length of paper clip		
Length of another object		

from your Desk or Notebook II

Use your 10cm or 1m tape.
Measure each object.

	estimate	actual
Length of a crayon		
Width of an eraser		
Length of a notebook		
Width of a notebook		
Length of a pencil		
Length of another object		

CURVY OBJECTS

Use your 10cm tape.
Measure each.

	estimate	actual
Around a dime		
Around a pencil		
Around a paper clip		
Around a pen		
Around another small object		

Task Cards for Make Your Own Measuring Tape

Teaching Aid 8.1b

From Exploring Mathematics: Activities for Concept and Skill Development, Copyright © 1990 Scott, Foresman and Company.

Thermometer Model

100°
90°
80°
70°
60°
50°
40°
30°
20°
10°
0°
-10°
-20°

From Exploring Mathematics: Activities for Concept and Skill Development, Copyright © 1990 Scott, Foresman and Company.

Teaching Aid 8.2

TEMPERATURE
Scavenger Hunt

30°C

Use the thermometer and find the temperature for each condition listed below. For most measurements, leave the thermometer at least 60 seconds, then read it quickly. Use the cooking or lab thermometer for temperatures you think will be above 50°C.

Location	Estimated Temperature	Actual Temperature
Outdoors	_____	_____
Indoors	_____	_____
Drinking fountain water	_____	_____
Tap water "hot"	_____	_____
"cold"	_____	_____
10 cm above the hot plate	_____	_____
In ice water		
In ice container	_____	_____
_____	_____	_____
_____	_____	_____
Your choices		
_____	_____	_____
_____	_____	_____

Teaching Aid 8.3

SHRINK-A-SHAPE

Cut a large simple shape from styrofoam.

Color it with markers.

Bake your shape in a toaster oven (150°C) on a baking sheet covered with foil.

Let your shape cool several seconds.

Remove it from the foil. The shape will be smaller and harder than the original.

SHRINK-A-SHAPE

Cut out a 10cm by 10cm square of styrofoam. Measure its depth in millimeters. Record its depth here. _____

Color and shrink your square according to the recipe. Sketch it below. Record its dimensions near the sketch.

length _____
width _____
depth _____

Cut out another shape. Sketch it below. Record at least 3 measurements on the sketch. Now shrink the shape. Sketch it after shrinking. Record its measurements.

Make some fractional statements about your shapes.